General editor: Graham Hand

Brodie's Notes on D. H. Lawrence's

The Rainbow

W. S. Bunnell

First published 1978 by Pan Books Ltd

This revised edition published 1993 by
THE MACMILLAN PRESS LTD
Houndmills, Basingstoke, Hampshire RG21 2XS
and London
Companies and representatives
throughout the world

ISBN 0-333-58142-3

Typeset by Footnote Graphics, Warminster, Wiltshire
Printed in Great Britain by
Cox & Wyman Ltd, Reading

Contents

Preface

The intention throughout this study aid is to stimulate and guide, to encourage your involvement in the book, and to develop informed responses and a sure understanding of the main details.

Brodie's Notes provide a clear outline of the play or novel's plot, followed by act, scene, or chapter summaries and/or commentaries. These are designed to emphasize the most important literary and factual details. Poems, stories or non-fiction texts combine brief summary with critical commentary on individual aspects or common features of the genre being examined. Textual notes define what is difficult or obscure and emphasize literary qualities. Revision questions are set at appropriate points to test your ability to appreciate the prescribed book and to write accurately and relevantly about it.

In addition, each of these Notes includes a critical appreciation of the author's art. This covers such major elements as characterization, style, structure, setting and themes. Poems are examined technically – rhyme, rhythm, for instance. In fact, any important aspect of the prescribed work will be evaluated. The aim is to send you back to the text you are studying.

Each study aid concludes with a series of general questions which require a detailed knowledge of the book: some of these questions may invite comparison with other books, some will be suitable for coursework exercises, and some could be adapted to work you are doing on another book or books. Each study aid has been adapted to meet the needs of the current examination requirements. They provide a basic, individual and imaginative response to the work being studied, and it is hoped that they will stimulate you to acquire disciplined reading habits and critical fluency.

Graham Handley 1990

The careful reading and rereading of the novel is the student's primary task. These notes are designed to increase the understanding and appreciation of the novel; they in no way provide a substitute for familiarity with it.

Page references in these Notes are to the Penguin edition of *The Rainbow*, but as references are also made to individual chapters, the Notes may be used with any edition of the book.

The author and his work

The biography of D. H. Lawrence is tremendously significant in reaching a full understanding of his work, which is an expression of his life, his feelings, his ideas and his relationships. He makes no attempt to be objective in his presentation of character, in the description of events, or in the development of his ideas.

David Herbert Lawrence was born on 11 September 1885 in a small house, part shop, in Eastwood, a mining village on the borders of Nottinghamshire and Derbyshire. Although the village was ugly, the countryside was near, and the district comprised a farming as well as a mining community.

Lawrence's father was a miner, almost illiterate and of inferior social status to his wife Lydia, who was better educated, read a good deal and was interested in ideas. She had been attracted by the virility and strength of her husband. They were an ill-matched pair and in constant conflict. Five children were born to them, and the children grew up in an atmosphere of quarrelling and hostility. His mother, a life-long teetotaller, would drive her husband into a rage by her attacks on him for wasting the family money on drink, often after a night at the pub where he sought the comfort, warmth and friendship which were denied to him at home.

Mrs Lawrence was determined that her children should not sink into their working-class background, and in this she succeeded, especially with Ernest, the second son, who worked in the London office of a shipping firm. Success in business was her ideal for her sons.

When Lawrence was twelve he gained a scholarship to Nottingham High School. At first he hated the cramping discipline of school, but, unlike Tom Brangwen, he attained a fair measure of academic success. On leaving school he was appointed as a clerk with a firm of surgical goods manu-facturers in Nottingham. He hated it. After three months an attack of pneumonia effected his escape.

One important influence in Lawrence's youth was the Con-gregational Church. Their mother insisted that the family attended church three times every Sunday and made them join the Band of Hope. This was the basis of the puritanism and earnestness which marked Lawrence's moral attitudes in later life. He was to adopt some strange gods, but his need for and approach to them was conditioned by the fierce non-conformity of his youth.

The death of Ernest in London was a shattering blow to his mother. It was only the necessity of nursing Lawrence in his illness that revived her interest in life. All the intensity of her love and ambition was now centred upon her younger son. It was to be a heavy cross for him to bear in spite of his deep and abiding love for her. *Sons and Lovers* was the fruit of this love and conflict.

After his illness, possibly warned by the doctor of the danger of tuberculosis, Lawrence did not return to work. Much of his time was spent at The Haggs, the farm of the Chambers family where Lawrence was always welcome. With Jessie Chambers he had a long emotional friendship, hovering on the brink often of a deeper and lasting relationship, a source of suffering as well as joy to both of them. Jessie is the Miriam of *Sons and Lovers*. In his excursions to the farm he was able to fulfil his love of natural things; his experiences there found expression in his first novel, *The White Peacock*, in *Sons and Lovers* and in parts of *The Rainbow*. His mother hated the influence of the farm in general and of Jessie in particular. Yet they were important elements in Lawrence's full development. The farm and the mine are the two poles around which much of Lawrence's work and ideas revolve.

In 1902 Lawrence went as a pupil–teacher to the British School in Eastwood. He did outstandingly well in the King's

Scholarship Examination, and in 1906 he began a two-year teacher training course at Nottingham University. For so many working-class boys of that time training for teaching provided the education that they needed to escape from their background.

In 1908 he became a teacher at Davidson Road School, Croydon, Surrey. At first, as with school and his first job, he hated it; yet he became a competent teacher. Sometimes he loved the work and the children, sometimes he loathed them.

> What does it matter to me, if they can write
> A description of a dog, or if they can't,

he wrote in one poem.

It was through Jessie Chambers's efforts that his first poems were published in the *English Review*. *The White Peacock* was published in 1911. Lawrence was able to show an advance copy to his mother just before she died of cancer. Her death left a great emptiness in his life. In spite of his relationship with Jessie Chambers and one or two abortive emotional relationships with other girls, his whole life had been bound up in his love for his mother, and her death left him rudderless and miserable. Lawrence's sister Emily said, 'Our Bert can never love any woman. He could only love his mother.' That may have been true of this period; some critics have attempted to prove it was true of Lawrence throughout his life. The evidence of his relationship to his wife Frieda makes manifest nonsense of such a contention.

In November 1911 tubercular pneumonia attacked both his lungs. He had to give up teaching and he applied for extended leave of absence. He never returned. For the rest of his life he was to depend on his writing, which often supplied the means for only a precarious existence. It also gave him the freedom to travel and this he did for the remainder of his life, never permanently settling in one place or one country.

Lawrence decided in 1912 to go to Germany. In an attempt to get a lectureship, he sought the support of Professor Ernest Weekley of Nottingham University. Thus he met Frieda, Professor Weekley's wife and the mother of three young children. She came from a German aristocratic family, the von Richthofens. Her father, Baron von Richthofen, was a professional soldier. She and Lawrence fell passionately and irrevocably in love. When they met Lawrence was twenty-six; she was thirty-one. Soon they were travelling together on the Continent, although they were not married until after Frieda's divorce in 1914. Frieda said of those days: 'I didn't want people, I didn't want anything, I only wanted to revel in this new world that Lawrence had given me.' The relationship was a stormy one, even at times violent. Yet of their need for each other there could be no doubt. Sometimes they found it difficult to live together; Frieda's aristocratic self-will was matched by Lawrence's own conviction that a right relationship between man and woman must be based on the woman's recognition of male mastery. Frieda was sometimes bitter about her children whom she was not allowed to see and Lawrence was at times intensely jealous of her longing to see them.

This period of his early relationship with Frieda was a fruitful one for his writing. They lived an isolated and solitary life in Gargnano near the Austro-Italian frontier on Lake Garda. During this time Lawrence completed the final revision of *Sons and Lovers* and wrote early versions of *The Rainbow, The Lost Girl*, parts of *Twilight in Italy* and some poems. Much of the housework in these early days was done by Lawrence, as Frieda was completely inexperienced in domestic work. In 1913 they moved to Bavaria where they lived in a house in the forest belonging to one of Frieda's relatives. Here the writing of *The Rainbow* continued. 'I know I can write bigger stuff than any man in England,' he said at this time. *The Rainbow* was then entitled *The Sisters*.

The publication of *Sons and Lovers* in 1913 established

Lawrence as an important writer. During brief visits to London he began to make the acquaintance of the literary society of the time – Edward Marsh, Cynthia Asquith, Katherine Mansfield and John Middleton Murry, with whom Lawrence was to have a stormy friendship, sometimes affectionate, sometimes verging on hatred, for the rest of his days. Murry figured largely in Lawrence's idea, his 'pet scheme', of forming a new community dedicated to living a life of individual fulfilment and a general acceptance of common ideals which, of course, were always those formulated by Lawrence and which changed startlingly from time to time. The only common factor in Lawrence's ideas was not their substance but the dogmatic fervour with which they were held.

The outbreak of the war meant that Lawrence had to live in England. He was, of course, with his tuberculosis, unfit for military service. They lived in various places – Greatham, Hampstead, Cornwall and Derbyshire; he and Frieda were hounded out of Cornwall on suspicion of being spies.

The Rainbow was published in September 1915. It was immediately attacked. 'Tedious and nauseating', 'a monotonous wilderness of phallicism', were words used by *The Daily News*. Soon police court proceedings were instituted against the book where it was described as – 'a mass of obscenity of thought, idea and action'. The book was ordered to be destroyed and Methuen, the publishers, were fined ten guineas. The defence of the book had been mishandled. Lawrence had no direct knowledge of the action. In spite of his assumed indifference he was shocked by the insult to the book, and, of course, it meant financially that the work on *The Rainbow* had been a waste of time.

However, by June 1916 he was working hard on *Women in Love*, a sort of sequel to *The Rainbow*; in Lawrence's judgement they were his two best books. At the end of the war he moved to Florence and later Sicily. This period, like the first in Italy, was a fruitful one, and led to the publication of

Aaron's Rod, a novel, *England, My England*, a book of short stories, and some poetry. Work on *Women in Love* continued; it was published in 1920. Lawrence called it 'a sequel to *The Rainbow* though quite unlike it'. In it he satirized many of his former friends. No one was exempt. Even Lawrence himself is satirized in the character of Birkin, who, on the one side, had 'a wonderful, desirable life-rapidity' but who, on the other, had 'this ridiculous mean effacement into a Salvator Mundi and a Sunday-school teacher, a prig of the stiffest type'.

This novel was very different in feeling and outlook from *The Rainbow*. A world war separated the world of *The Rainbow* from that of *Women in Love*. There had been many changes in the world and in Lawrence's own outlook. *Women in Love* stemmed, of course, from the original *The Two Sisters*; Ursula and Gudrun appear in both books. There is still the same basic Lawrentian plot of the study and working out of a relationship between different sets of people. The canvas of *Women in Love* is wider than that in *The Rainbow*. Yet together they constitute, in their different ways, great works. 'These two books would by themselves have been enough to place Lawrence among the greatest English writers,' wrote Mr F. R. Leavis.

The Lost Girl was finally published in 1920. It was intended to be a popular novel; certainly it ranks among the lowest of all Lawrence's works. Ironically it was awarded the James Tait Black Memorial Prize.

In 1922 Lawrence left Europe, first of all to go to Australia which aroused in him a strange mixture of liking and dislike. His experiences there inspired the novel *Kangaroo*, published in 1923, and *The Boy in the Bush*, published in 1924 and written in collaboration with M. L. Skinner. As well as the usual study in a man–woman relationship, *Kangaroo* is also a venture into the world of politics. It is artistically not one of Lawrence's most successful novels in spite of the vivid picture he creates of Australia. *The Boy in the Bush* is the story of a young Englishman's relations with women set in a historical background.

From Australia Lawrence went to Mexico, where his mystical religious zeal found the inspiration for the novel, *The Plumed Serpent*, an attempt to examine relationships in terms of a primitive symbolism.

In 1923 Lawrence was back in London, miserable but full of plans still for establishing his new community. Finally he set out with only one disciple, Dorothy Brett, a convinced and unswerving admirer of everything connected with Lawrence. Lawrence, Frieda and Dorothy Brett went first to New York, then to Chicago and on to Taos. In New Mexico Lawrence led a life close to the soil, building and farming. During this time, he was also occupied in writing *The Plumed Serpent*. Frieda grew tired of the triangle of Lawrence, herself and Dorothy Brett, and he finally sent Dorothy off to Mexico.

The tuberculosis from which Lawrence had always suffered was getting worse. He knew that not much time was left for him, even though he refused to admit how serious his state was. The doctors in Mexico City warned Frieda that he had only a year or two to live. In fact he had five years. In 1925 he was too ill to travel to England. At the Del Monte Ranch Lawrence recovered and the horrors of his serious illness in Mexico City were forgotten in his return to his country pursuits.

In September 1925, he was well enough to sail from New York for Southampton. On his return he went by car round his native Derbyshire, and the idea for *Lady Chatterley's Lover*, his last novel, was born. He and Frieda then went to a villa at Spotorno on the Italian Riviera. There Lawrence worked on two long short stories, *The Virgin and the Gipsy* and *Glad Ghosts*. The visit of Frieda's daughters aroused Lawrence's jealousy. The situation between Frieda and Lawrence was aggravated by the presence of his sister Ada who encouraged his bitterness against Frieda. They then moved into a Tuscan Farm near Florence where Lawrence wrote little. In the autumn of 1926 he renewed his friendship with Aldous Huxley, who portrayed Lawrence happily in *Two or Three Graces* and later as Rampion in *Point Counter Point*.

In 1926 Lawrence visited England for the last time. Back in Italy at Scandicci he began *Lady Chatterley's Lover*, in which he was to see sexual harmony and fulfilment as an antidote to industrial ugliness. He also worked on *Etruscan Places*, the last of the travel books. In the summer of 1927 he had a serious lung haemorrhage. He was engaged in preparing *Lady Chatterley's Lover* for publication by an Italian printer, in spite of the furore he knew it would create. He also planned an exhibition of his pictures at Dorothy Warren's art gallery. When the exhibition finally opened after many delays, it was an outstanding success. However, the Home Secretary ordered the removal of thirteen of the pictures, together with some reproductions, and, amazingly enough, a volume of William Blake's drawings.

> Virginal, pure policemen came
> and hid their faces for very shame,
> while they carried the shameless things away
> to gaol, to be hid from the light of day

was Lawrence's comment on the incident.

Lady Chatterley's Lover could not be prosecuted in the courts as *The Rainbow* had been, but the Customs were diligent in their attempt to ensure that it did not circulate freely. Lawrence travelled in Switzerland, Austria and the South of France in a desperate attempt to find suitable places in different seasons to live with his tuberculosis in some degree of comfort.

When Lawrence came to Bandol in the South of France in September 1929, he was dying. Yet he was still able to enjoy the beauty of the Mediterranean. He could no longer work. A specialist who came out from England advised his removal to a sanatorium at Vence. He hated hospital, as long ago he had hated school. In March he was moved to a villa nearby. To the last he needed Frieda and demanded her constant presence. He died on 2 March 1930.

It is ironic that Lawrence, with his belief in vitality, in the mere joy of living and the glory of the flesh, should have died so young.

'For man,' as he wrote, 'the vast marvel is to be alive ... Whatever the unborn and the dead may know, they cannot know the beauty, the marvel of being alive in the flesh ... We ought to dance with rapture that we should be alive and in the flesh, and part of the living, incarnate cosmos.'

Chapter summaries, critical commentary, textual notes and revision questions

Chapter 1

1 The Brangwen family had lived for generations on the Marsh Farm, situated on the Derbyshire–Nottinghamshire border, two miles from the church-tower at Ilkeston. They were blond people, slow in speech, with an expectant air. They were neither rich nor poor. They were close to the land and worked hard on it. The women's horizons were wider than the men's; they demanded more than the 'blood-intimacy' of creation. Mrs Brangwen looked to the vicar and the squire's lady, like the other women in the village, to represent another form of life, different and superior.

2 A canal is built across the Brangwen land; the railway comes and collieries are developed. But the farm remains separate. Alfred Brangwen has married a woman who sometimes criticizes her husband and everyone else. Alfred does as he likes and laughs at her criticism. They are at once together and separate. Four sons and two daughters are born to them. Tom is the youngest. At the Grammar School, although he tries hard, he gains little success. He enjoys the friendships he makes, but he is glad to leave, to get back to the farm. His father breaks his neck on the farm when Tom is seventeen. He takes over the care of the farm, gets drunk sometimes and once goes with a prostitute. This upsets his concept of the woman as the representative of high morality, founded on the part played in the house by his mother and sister. His mother dies when he is twenty-three. He drinks a lot, and has sexual experience with a girl he meets casually on a day out. When her own man, a foreigner, turns up, Brangwen is more fascinated by him than by the girl. He feels an intense desire to marry, but he wants none of the girls whom he meets. Heavy drinking assuages his restlessness and quenches his individuality. When he is twenty-eight, he meets a woman who is housekeeper to the vicar. She is Polish with a young child. She is the daughter of a landowner and has been married before. They visit the farm, and Tom becomes more fascinated by her. Finally he goes to the vicarage to propose marriage to her and, although she is older than Tom, she accepts him. Even at the time of his proposal, he is overwhelmed by the sensations of closeness and separation.

Note the directness of the description, which is endowed with poetic qualities and conveys a sense of history, the passage of time: it is full of rhythmic innovations, cumulative repetitions since life itself and the living of life are repetitive. Class differences are spelled out too. There is a strong sense of the spiritual, and of the need for education so that the other language — that of the vicar, for example, may be mastered — and the role model of Mrs Hardy is important in firing ambition.

The historical emphasis, here a deliberate retrospect, is used by Lawrence to authenticate the medium in which his characters move and have their being. Family history is detailed too, so that one is aware of the continuum in families, the repetition of certain traits through the generations. Soon the focus sharpens to Tom. His frustrating experience with the prostitute is prelude to his fuller recognition in himself of the need for sexual fulfilment, but he is essentially modest and conventional in his attitude towards the role of the woman. Most interesting is the experience with the girl he picks up: after his satisfaction he contemplates the foreigner whose mistress she is, and realizes from the man's inscrutable sophistication that there is a different life from the one he leads and knows about. After his periods at the Red Lion there are drinking bouts of greater intensity, an indication of his inability to find fulfilment at any depth in life. There follows his first glimpse of Anna Lensky, his intuitive recognition that she is the woman for him, and then the superb interaction with Tilly — here we note the realism of the dialogue. From now on there is a wonderful intensity in the writing — the language of the child naturally conveyed, the visit of the woman to borrow (it is almost as if fate has conspired to put her in Brangwen's way), the first moving communication between him and the Polish lady. Brangwen's reactions are probed, his consciousness revealed to the reader: there is an instinctual recognition between the man and the woman, existing on an emotional level and recognition which they cannot easily articulate. Brangwen's tension as he puts on his clean shirt to go and propose to her is excellently conveyed. The scene in which he watches the mother and her child is graphic with the intensity of his feeling and the separateness of their world. Note the directness of Brangwen's proposal, and the equally direct response of the woman — the whole scene is limpid with emotional and sexual feeling. But there is more than this — Lawrence employs Biblical rhythms to suggest that this recognition and coming together has a spiritual quality too. But the parting carries another kind of recognition — her foreignness, their different lives. His reflexes as he leaves show Lawrence with his character in his intimate feelings. One of the great strengths of *The Rainbow* is the depth of emotional identification with character in action and inter- action.

The Brangwens ... Farm The matter-of-fact opening is in direct contrast to the rising imaginative language as the section develops.

expecting something unknown This would be an approximate description of Lawrence's own personality and approach.

blood flowed heavy This is typical of Lawrence's style and emotion, and is repeated in phrases like 'blood-intimacy' and 'pulsing heat of creation'.

Odyssey An epic poem by the ancient Greek poet Homer

describing the adventures of Ulysses returning home from the Trojan Wars to his wife Penelope.

Circe Renowned for her magic art, Circe dwelt on an island on which Ulysses was cast. Ulysses' companions were changed into swine when they drank from the magic cup that Circe offered them. Penelope, whilst Ulysses was away, held off her importunate suitors by saying that she would not give an answer until she had finished a robe she was making. She unravelled every night the work she had done during the day.

safe side of civilization It was the encroaching of industry on the countryside that oppressed Lawrence. The position of the Marsh Farm is not dissimilar to The Haggs where much of Lawrence's boyhood and youth was passed.

Grammar School in Derby Tom like Lawrence goes to grammar school. Lawrence also hated his school, but he certainly had more academic ability than Tom.

sensuously developed Like Lawrence himself.

Tennyson's Ulysses Alfred Tennyson (1809–92) was perhaps the most successful of all Victorian poets. *Ulysses* is a poem about the aged Ulysses setting out to seek new adventures, and is characterized by Tennyson's mastery of the verbal music of poetry.

Shelley Percy Bysshe Shelley (1792–1822) was a Romantic poet whose work was noted for its lyricism.

Oh wild west ... being From Shelley's *Ode to the West Wind*.

bowels A source of intense emotion for Lawrence, to which he often refers.

consumptive type Like Lawrence himself who suffered and finally died from tuberculosis.

mardy Soft, spoilt (dialect).

Prometheus Bound A tragedy by the ancient Greek writer Aeschylus. Prometheus, the champion of mankind, was chained to a rock by Jupiter.

nice girl Lawrence himself found the same inhibitions, symbolized in his relationship to Jessie Chambers, the Miriam of *Sons and Lovers*.

His mother died For Tom this is not quite the catastrophic event that it was for Lawrence or for Paul Morel in *Sons and Lovers*. Nevertheless he is left with a sense of emptiness and lack of purpose, which are resolved only, when like Lawrence, he finds a woman to love utterly.

Brangwen loved the other man ... graciousness This exemplifies Lawrence's abiding preoccupation with the

relationships between man and man as well as with man and
woman, woman and woman (Ursula and Winifred).

britching Pushing backwards. This is from breeching, which
refers to the strong leather strap passing round the breech of a
shaft horse, and enabling the horse to push backwards.

foreigner Like Lawrence's wife Frieda von Richthofen, who was
German, also of 'superior birth' and older than Lawrence.

Chapter 2

Lydia Lensky's father was a Polish landowner, married to a
German wife. He was constantly in debt. She had married a
young doctor by whom she had had two children who died.
Her husband was a convinced patriot who swept her along in
his intensity. After the great rebellion they had to flee to
London. Lensky's spirit was destroyed. When their child
Anna was born he was dying. After his death, she nursed an
old rector in his house on the Yorkshire coast. She was conscious of little except vaguely of the changing patterns of
nature. When he died, she moved to Cossethay where she
meets Tom Brangwen. Her body responds to his presence; she
knows he can awaken her. Before her marriage she goes
through moods of want, rejection and indifference to Tom,
and he suffers in these changes. In marriage, Tom finds a new
certainty in life; he lives by her. Their relationship is securely
based in physical communion. He works hard to gain Anna's
affection, and finally succeeds. When Lydia is pregnant she
withdraws from Tom. He is angry and overwhelmed. He
spends the night of his wife's labour comforting the distraught
Anna.

The retrospect is important to our understanding of Lydia
and emphatic of the totally different background which has
shaped her. Note the death of her two young children, and in
fact her association with death which so influences her life.
Lawrence emphasizes that the past is always present in her,
and this is why at times she is withdrawn from Tom Bran-

gwen. Lyrical and natural description accompany their coming together, their responses to each other given a poetic quality. But Lawrence also stresses the withdrawals which so reduce Brangwen. After the marriage the differences still remain, but Lawrence's description of their day-to-day life is informed with intimate knowledge. Lydia's stories further emphasize the divisions, but Lawrence describes the periods of conflict and the periods of ecstasy which constitute their reality. We recognize the truth of the relationship, the new separation when she becomes pregnant and Brangwen seems shut off from her. But perhaps the finest parts of this chapter deal with Brangwen's relationship with Anna. Lawrence is superbly the analyst of a child's mind – the exchanges are full of pathos, often of humour, and always have a convincing truth to human nature. Both dialogue and description – visual movements of Anna, for example – are captured. Even better is the farm description, with its earthy and poetic qualities intermixed, as in reality. The birth pangs lead to a more complete relationship between Anna and her stepfather: the tenderness he displays is a caring which is in part the result of not being able to come to terms with his wife's suffering in labour. It is significant that he puts Anna in his old room. The chapter ends movingly with the words which place the characters against the infinitude of life – 'The swift unseen threshing of the night upon him silenced him and he was overcome. He turned away indoors, humbly. There was the infinite world, eternal, unchanging, as well as the world of life'. It is a typical Lawrentian perspective.

nothing ... eyes This was a feature that friends often noted about Lawrence himself.

great ideas Lensky's own Messianic sense of mission might be compared to Lawrence's own, except Lensky's found expression in action, Lawrence's only in his writing.

parturition The words and images connected with procreation are an important element in creating the atmosphere of this chapter.

Gethsemane ... Triumphal Entry Gethsemane is situated on the Mount of Olives, east of Jerusalem, and is the garden in which Judas is supposed to have betrayed Christ. The Triumphal Entry is that of Christ into Jerusalem (Mark 11, 1–12). The use of these terms is an indication of the equating of the relationship of man and woman to religion.

gouvernante A governess.

Yiddish The old German language, with many borrowings from other languages, spoken by Jews in Eastern Europe.

great, yellow moon hanging heavy All nature seems to take on the qualities of the pregnant woman.

Chapter 3

The relationship between Tom and Anna blossoms. With the birth of a son to Tom and Lydia, Anna loses her jealous protective attitude towards her mother. Tom is jealous of his own child and its relationship to Lydia and his love goes out to Anna. They go everywhere together, even to the cattle-market. Tom visits his brother's mistress, and this leads to a discussion of his relationship with Lydia. They are aware of their increasing estrangement, but, when she comes to him, they find a new and deeper love for each other. Strangers on one level, they yet have this enduring bond springing out of physical communion.

This is a moving and convincing chapter which traces the mutuality of love between Tom and Anna – warm, tremulous, possessive. Although the sexual passion between Tom and Lydia remains strong and fulfilling, he is aware of her separateness and acknowledges his own jealousy of the baby. Lawrence captures perfectly the jokes and rows between Tom and Anna, the driving in the trap is expressive of their need for each other's companionship, Anna's sharpness in the pub and at market a source of delight to Tom. Such is his love and pride that Lawrence tells us 'There grew in Brangwen's heart now a secret desire to make her a lady': this cunningly represents his wish to see her equivalent to her mother, but in his own English society. After his visit to Alfred and his meeting with Mrs Forbes Tom becomes aware of his own lack of culture. He is restless at home but Lydia, aware of his reactions, moves him to a fuller consummation with her. Once again the Biblical imagery is used to reinforce the conception. Anna 'played between the pillar of fire and the pillar of cloud in confidence'. The chapter ends with an extension of the image which resonates with the title of the novel – 'her father and her mother now met to the span of the heavens, and she, the child, was free to play in the space beneath, between'. Note the repetition, which here reflects the rhythm of life.

jealous of the child Although childless himself, Lawrence was intensely jealous of Frieda's longing for her children by her former marriage.

fawce Cunning, sharp (dialect).

Herbert Spencer Herbert Spencer (1820–1903) was a writer concerned with social and political philosophy.

Browning Robert Browning (1812–89) was, with Tennyson, the greatest of the Victorian poets. His poetry is marked by psychological analysis, strange characterization, and sometimes passion.

chilling about her Lawrence disliked intellectual women – those who, according to him, had 'sex in the head'. The quick summing up of character in this brief paragraph is typical of Lawrence's ability to describe a character briefly and effectively both in his novels and in life.

God was her father and her mother Again this reveals Lawrence's religious approach.

Chapter 4

When she is nine, Anna goes to school. She is shy yet aggressive; her life and emotions are firmly centred on her mother and father. When she is ten she and her mother go to stay with the Baron Skrebensky, the unhappy, exiled Polish aristocrat, now vicar of a large parish in the North of England. Anna is impressed by him. When she goes to school in Nottingham, she feels a sense of separateness from its social life and of futility in much of its teaching. At seventeen she is moody and unpredictable, closer to her father than to her mother. Her cousin Will begins to visit the Marsh when he starts work in Ilkeston as a draughtsman. She giggles at his loud singing in church, but is impressed by his talk of church architecture. Love grows between them, and, in spite of Will's lack of money, they are to be married just before Christmas. Tom Brangwen feels rejected. However, when they obtain a cottage, he delights in buying Anna gadgets for it.

The focus is very much on the character of Anna and her development. Lawrence says that in Cossethay 'she was always an alien', and we note her impressionability when she goes to meet the Baron and how his image remains in her memory. Part of Anna's separateness is shown in her rejection of common people. She is socially ambitious, aware of the limitations of her family, interacting aggressively with her father, particularly when he drinks. We also register her spiritual capacity which 'worshipped God as a mystery', and her teenage years, with the anxiety to leave home, are convincingly chronicled by Lawrence. Particularly good is her reception of her cousin Will, and her laughing at him because of his voice – this does much to humanize her on a commonplace level – but Will is instrumental in expanding her horizons through his knowledge of church architecture. Their love is passionately, movingly and poetically conveyed. *The Rainbow* is a novel about the generations of a family, and we feel here the connection with Lydia and Tom, the irony being that of course Anna is now beginning to reject her parents, particularly the 'father' who has been so close to her. Tom's feelings are poignantly conveyed. Lawrence puts the conflict within him well – 'And a black gloom of anger, and a tenderness of self-effacement, fought in his heart'. The woodcarving of Adam and Eve has a strong symbolic effect in the context of the novel – another Biblical reinforcement of the theme which links the instinctive and the spiritual in man and woman. The gathering of the sheaves and Anna's reactions afterwards – and Will's – also have a lyrical quality, a symbolic expression in nature of their physical passion. When Tom gives Will the money for the shares, Anna's reaction is passionately to clasp her father and call him Daddy once again. Brangwen knows instinctively the truth – 'The child who clung to him wanted her child-husband'. Lawrence's insight into the intimacy of family relations and the beginnings of passionate love is nowhere better exemplified than in this chapter.

dame's school A village school run by one teacher.

Baron Skrebensky The Skrebensky family appear from time to time in the novel, leading up to Ursula's relationship with Anton Skrebensky.

Alexandra, Princess of Wales Alexandra (1844–1925), later Queen Consort, was the wife of Edward VII. She was a Danish princess and known for her beauty and her dignity.

Goose Fair A fair once held in many English towns at Michaelmas (29 September) when geese were plentiful. The most famous was that held at Nottingham.

gaucherie Awkwardness in manners (French).

Ave Maria Hail Mary, a prayer (Latin).

Pater Noster Our Father (Latin). Used also to refer to the small and large beads of the rosary.

Ave Maria ... nostrae Hail Mary, full of grace, the Lord is with thee, blessed art thou amongst women, blessed is the fruit of thy womb, Jesus. Holy Mary, Mother of God, pray for us sinners now and at the hour of our death.

torture cell Such cells were built with conical floors like an inverted sugar loaf. There were two in existence under the ecclesiastical jurisdiction of Paris, at the Grand Châtelot and at the Bastille. In the Tower of London they were called cells of 'Little Ease'.

Ruskin John Ruskin (1819–1900) wrote on painting and architecture, including *The Seven Lamps of Architecture* and *The Stones of Venice*. Ruskin advocated Gothic architecture as a style.

nave The main part of a church to the choir.

chancel East end of a church reserved for choir and clergy.

transept Transverse part of a church built in the form of a cross.

rood-screen Carved screen, often in wood, separating the nave from the choir.

Norman hatchet carving Anglo-Saxon and early Norman masons used an axe to carve rough ornamentation.

Gothic A style of medieval architecture, marked by the use of the pointed arch, narrow windows, and conspicuous spires.

Renaissance The revival of classical styles in architecture – and also art and literature. It began in Italy in the fourteenth century.

Perpendicular A form of Gothic, marked by the use of the vertical line, especially in window and wall tracing. It flourished from about 1350–1500.

Early English A form of Gothic, developed from the Norman period of architecture. This early thirteenth-century movement marked the foundation of a specifically English Architecture in which the round arch was superseded by the pointed arch and other features of the Gothic style.

Norman A type of architecture noted for its general massiveness of design and use of the round arch. It flourished about 1050–1200.

Southwell In Nottinghamshire. Southwell is one of the smaller and least known of the English cathedrals. It has a Norman front.

sedilia Set of three stone seats for priests in the south wall of the chancel.

phoenix A mythological bird, the only one of its kind, which renewed itself from the ashes of its own funeral pile. It was used as an emblem by Lawrence himself and placed over his grave.

moon The moon has an important influence on characters in the novel. 'The Moon is the centre of our terrestrial individuality in the cosmos. She is the declaration of our existence in separateness,' wrote Lawrence in *Fantasia of the Unconscious*.

staved Made of curved pieces of wood.

Chapter 5

Anna and Will are married. At the marriage party, Tom makes a speech about the importance of marriage. The men sing carols as Will and Anna settle down in bed.

This short chapter is a brilliant – and often humorous – description of the wedding. Tom's speech is punctuated by

interruptions, and we feel throughout the truth of the dialogue
to the situation. There is a poignancy about the family ser-
enading the newly-marrieds with hymns, and even as she
swoons into her new life, Anna can hear the voice of her father
'singing with gusto'. The register is that of change: Tom
Brangwen has come through the crisis of what he feels is
rejection, and Anna has come to the natural consummation of
love.

wake A group of festival merry-makers.
guysers Sometimes spelt 'guisers', those in 'disguise' or
masquerade dress.
mystery play A play dealing with incidents from the Gospels or
the legends of saints.
Beelzebub Prince of the devils.

Revision questions on chapters 1–5

1 Trace the stages in the development of Tom Brangwen's
relationship to Lydia.

2 How far is Tom's speech on marriage at Anna's wedding
the result of his own experiences?

3 Describe the growth of the relationship between Tom and
Anna.

4 How important an influence is Lydia's foreign
background both in her relationship to Tom and in her own
development?

Chapter 6

Anna and Will spend their honeymoon in the cottage. They
are utterly absorbed in each other and feel completely
divorced from the outside world. Will is vaguely troubled
when they stay in bed together at all times; Anna exults in it.
When Tom Brangwen visits them he feels a glowing quality
about them. When they begin to return to everyday life, Anna

is irritated by Will hanging around her. He is moved to intense anger by her rejection. They develop alongside their love a frenzy of hatred for each other. Yet they know they cannot live without each other. Physical communion remains their supreme point of contact. They have different ways of looking at things, particularly in religion. He accepts things on an instinctual level; Anna wants to know the truth, the reality, the meaning of things. They begin to battle with each other for dominance; they make each other very unhappy. Will's attempts at mastery arouse Anna's contempt. Will's dark intensity kills the innocent radiant love in Anna. When Anna is pregnant she dances naked and alone. When Will sees her, he feels hurt and obliterated. She hates him for his hold over her and for his dependence on her. She is the centre and the circumference of his world. She refuses to sleep with him. At last he learns how to be alone; but he is still desolate and dependent on her. Friendship grows between them; but it is a lesser thing than their earlier relationship. When Ursula is born Anna feels triumphant. She is thrilled feeding the baby at her breast, and she loves her husband's body. Will is increasingly conscious that his whole life lies in Anna and in any children she may have. Yet Anna is not quite fulfilled. It is the knowledge that she is again pregnant that finally satisfies her and removes her discontent.

The whole of this chapter is a searching examination of the most intimate of relationships, here fictionalized but nonetheless essentially true in its emphasis. The main areas of togetherness and difference are given in the summary above, but note the intensity of the self-absorption which shuts out the world. For Lawrence an intimate relationship carried within it the seeds of conflict and even perhaps of self-destruction. The title of the chapter is in itself an indication of the terrible penalties of intimacy. Will finds the acceptance of change difficult, and the intensity of hatred in reaction is tellingly conveyed. The very closeness brings irritation and more, as well as the return to consummation. Note here the hawk–predator imagery which conveys via instinct the tenacity of the struggle and the will to tear and hurt as well as love. His interest in church architecture is his release, and Lawrence is preparing us for the fact that ultimately Will is to make his own career through his love of his art. The unevenness of their life is stressed, for each is adjusting to the new situation. Friction leaps violently to the fore. This is seen in his destruction of the Adam and Eve carving – it is a kind of self-destruction and humiliation really – and although Anna weeps for a day, she has won. Their separateness is seen with her knowledge that she is pregnant, her dancing registering a kind of primitive fulfilment, and her triumphant 'Anna Victrix' the possession of the child who sucks her. But there is a returning love and gratitude to the man who gave her the child – but as ever, Lawrence uses the fighting blue-tits as symbol, as record, of their own fights: Anna, despite the child, waxes restless for the unknown. But she comes to accept what she has. We are once more aware of the title of the novel as she contemplates her life: 'Dawn and sunset were the feet of the rainbow that spanned the day, and she saw the hope, the promise. Why should she travel any further?'. In fact she doesn't, giving herself up to family life and the bringing into that life of more children – 'She was a door and a threshhold, she herself. Through her another soul was coming, to stand upon her as upon the threshhold'.

hucksters Hawkers.
Tablets of Stone The Ten Commandments received from Jehovah by Moses.
Lord in two burning bushes Exodus 3, 2–5. Lawrence several times uses references to the burning bush.
fairy tale Probably a reference to *King for a Day* which appears in a selection *Eye of a God*, *Tales of East and West*, by W. A. Frazer, published in 1899.
illuminations in old missals The decorations in gold, silver and brilliant colours of the initial letters in old books of prayer.

Pietà The Virgin Mary holding the dead body of Christ on her lap.

Eucharist Lord's Supper.

Bamberg Cathedral A magnificent Byzantine-style cathedral situated in Bavaria, Germany.

Annunciation The Announcement made by the archangel Gabriel to the Virgin Mary that she was to be the mother of Christ.

water turned to wine at Cana John 2, 1–11.

oriflamme Sacred banner of Saint Dennis, made of red silk.

Magnificat Hymn of the Virgin Mary. 'My soul doth magnify the Lord ...' Luke, 1, 46–55.

Fra Angelico Guido di Pietro, known as Fra Angelico (1387–1455), an Italian painter.

David who danced before the Lord II Samuel 6, 14.

Michal II Samuel 6, 16. Michal, the daughter of Saul, looked out of the window, and saw King David leaping and dancing before the Lord; and she despised him in her heart.

the Philistine, the Giant Goliath, the Philistine whom David slew. I Samuel 17.

the old man of the sea The old man of the sea hoisted himself on to the shoulders of Sinbad who was able to free himself only by getting the old man drunk.

Pisgah mount The mountain from which Moses was allowed a glimpse of the Promised Land before he died.

rainbow like an archway This makes an interesting comparison with Ursula's vision at the very end of the novel. It widens the meaning of the symbol, especially in its use by the earth-bound Anna.

Chapter 7

Anna and Will go to visit the Baron Skrebensky who has married a young English girl of good family after the death of his first wife. From the Skrebenskys', they visit Lincoln Cathedral. The Cathedral causes a sense of soaring excitement in Will. Anna is angered by his passion towards the Cathedral. She destroys all his feelings by drawing his attention to a little carved face. The local church is also a centre of love and interest for Will. He cares for the fabric and becomes choirmaster. Anna finds joy and satisfaction in the baby; Will serves the family.

The conflict continues in this chapter, with Anna tormenting her husband because of his absorption in the Cathedral. Lawrence is probing the continuum of the differences between them, and also the deep-rooted possessiveness of human nature. Despite her reaction, Anna is also exalted by the experience of the visit to the cathedral. In one magnificent paragraph ('Here the stone leapt from the plain of earth ...') Lawrence is equating once more spiritual and sexual consummation, even using the language of passion to convey it. The bitterness in Will as he hears Anna's comment on the carved face shows how Lawrence is aware of structural echoes in his novel ('This was the voice of the serpent in his Eden' – and remember he has destroyed his Adam and Eve). Will finds more than consolation in his experiences of nature after this – life always has its compensations – but he has 'relaxed his will, and let everything go'. His moods are gradually understood by Anna, and his work has to suffice him. He comes to know his own limitations.

God burned no more in that bush cf. the reference in Chapter 6.

Chapter 8

Will is deeply stirred by his relationship to Ursula. Anna, in her second child Gudrun, revels in the ecstasy of motherhood. Anna and Will remain separate by day but come together at night. Will loves to have Ursula near him, although at times he can turn upon her. Ursula lives for him and in his light. Gudrun follows Ursula's lead. By the time Will is twenty-six he and Anna have four children. Ursula remains deeply influenced by her father. The connection between them strengthens as she grows older. He has a perverse desire to frighten her and this leads to his doing daring things with her.

One night at the theatre Will picks up a young girl. Later in the park he makes love to her, although it is broken off before he possesses her. This leads to a new chapter in his relationship with Anna when they exploit fully the sensual pleasures that they can give each other. Will starts his handicraft classes in the evening.

The continuum in the generations is maintained by the stress on the developing relationship between Will and the baby Ursula (you might compare this with that of Tom and Anna). Will makes her his own. There is a spasm of jealousy from Anna, and we are soon made aware again of the power of possessiveness. There is a wonderful humour and understanding between father and daughter. But when he breaks into a rage – when he can't cope with something she has done, or is supposed to have done – we feel her hurt as the black temper comes upon him. But she has her own resistant self-absorption, a quality inherited from both her parents but more particularly from her mother. Lawrence is adept at indicating family consistency in this way. Anna, for example, has it in 'her trance of motherhood'. Lawrence balances this with some tender scenes, as when Ursula helps – almost hinders – her father with the planting of the potatoes. What Lawrence calls 'this curious taunting intimacy' between father and daughter is well illustrated by the incident on the swing-boats. The movement away from Anna is shown in the incident with the girl in Nottingham. It leads to deeper exploration and consummation with Anna, who can read his moods and his motivations, and can possess him at will. But Lawrence himself is exploring the conscious and subconscious levels of loving and intimacy, and rejecting by direct statement the concept of shame or any preconceived moral judgement.

spritted Sprouted.
Empire A music hall.
Swedish methods The Swedish approach to handwork

instruction sprang from a desire to perpetuate folk industries. Special schools and a teachers' centre were established. Many English teachers attended the summer schools which were held and a Teachers' Handbook was translated and published in England.

Chapter 9

Anna's two brothers, Tom and Fred, are now young men. Tom is intelligent but always set apart from the rest of mankind. Fred is a typical Brangwen, blue-eyed, large-boned and English. Tom, their father, becomes something of a gentleman farmer, content to leave the routine running of the farm to Fred. He is drowned when he is returning from a merry evening in Nottingham. He arrives home when the banks of the canal break, and he is engulfed in the flood water. Fred finds the dead body of his father, and it is taken to Anna's house to be laid out. Her father's death and funeral make Will love Anna even more. Lydia Brangwen finds her consolation in her grandchildren, especially in Ursula whose questions about her two grandfathers set Lydia thinking about her first husband and her life with him.

This is another account of the historical and personal in the Brangwen family. Note the way Lawrence creates atmosphere on the night of the tragedy of drowning, with Tom Brangwen convinced that he can deal with anything (including heavy rain) and then the graphic description of the horror as he chokes and his wife calling his name as she moves about the house. Lawrence does not go over the top in his descriptions – they are positive and evocative of place, sensation, response. When they get Brangwen's body out we read: 'Hay and twigs and dirt were in the beard and hair. The youth pushed through the water crying loudly without tears, like a stricken animal. The mother at the window cried, making no trouble'. Note the fine sense of related perspective. Ursula's glimpse of her Uncle Tom's silent grief in the garden is also vivid with actuality. Another fundamental truth is Will's response to the tragedy by being more fiercely in love with Anna, a reflex of natural intensity. The interaction between Ursula and her grandmother Lydia is redolent with truth, and another retrospect on Lydia's life, done convincingly from the standpoint of old age, is both moving and, for Ursula, disturbing as she contemplates the future.

Agnostic Agnostic was a word coined by T. H. Huxley in 1869 to describe the state of neither believing nor denying but remaining in a state of doubt until convincing proof or evidence could be found.

gig-lamps Lights on the two-wheeled one-horse carriage.

Chapter 10

Ursula finds being the eldest child in the family a heavy weight to carry. She and Gudrun continue in their close relationship, Ursula concerned with the real world, Gudrun with the life of the imagination. The Brangwen girls war with the boys of the Phillips family, and then adopt them as sweethearts. Ursula and Gudrun go to the Grammar School in Nottingham. The house remains a scene of bustling activity with many younger children who give Ursula little peace. Her relationship to her father is temporarily soured when he hits her across the face for leaving the door of the parish room unlocked. At school she is quick and intelligent, although sometimes rebellious and shy, exacting in the standards she expects of others. Gudrun makes little progress at school. Ursula is absorbed in questions of sin and the personality of Jesus. Christmas comes with its preparations and high expectations that wither as the day progresses.

Again the atmosphere of family life and its effect on the growing Ursula is convincingly conveyed. The different natures of Gudrun and Ursula are stressed, and the fights with other children have the authenticity of felt experience.

Ursula's otherness is explicitly defined, but the incident where her father hits her with the duster shows her extreme vulnerability. Her suffering is another change in their relationship – 'She no longer belonged to him unquestioned'. The delight in learning and her sense of superiority at the Grammar School show Lawrence fully entering into the consciousness and the experience of his character. Ursula has an acute social consciousness, as we see from the sensitivity she shows about the behaviour of the other children in public. Lawrence also traces with sensitive understanding the nature of her response to religion and faith – it is a phase in Ursula's life which is movingly recorded. And from time to time throughout this chapter as indeed throughout the novel we notice Lawrence's observations of nature: 'There was the wonderful, starry, straight track of a pheasant's footsteps across the snow, imprinted so clear; there the lobbing mark of the rabbit, two holes abreast, two holes following behind ...'. The description of the failed Christmas – failed 'because this day was become as every day' is a well-sustained rhetorical sequence from Lawrence on the contradictions and paradoxes of Christianity.

Andersen Hans Christian Andersen (1830–75), Danish writer, chiefly known for his fairy tales.

Grimm Two brothers, Jacob Ludwig Karl (1785–1863) and Wilhelm Karl (1786–1859), writers on German folklore, famous for their fairy tales.

Idylls of the King By Lord Tennyson. See note on Tennyson in Chapter 1. *Idylls of the King* are a series of poems telling the story of King Arthur and his Knights of the Round Table. The chief characters include Launcelot and Elaine. Astolat is now Guildford in Surrey.

Il était ... patapon 'There was a shepherdess, purr, purr, purr, little kitty.' From a traditional French song.

Samuel, Samuel! I Samuel 3, 4–10.

serpent Genesis 3.

Judas Judas betrayed Christ with a kiss and for money (thirty pieces of silver).

evangelical A section of Protestantism which asserts that salvation is through faith and words not through the sacraments.

Stigmata Marks made by the nails and the spear at the Crucifixion.

Calvary The scene of the Crucifixion.

The Sons of God ... of renown Genesis 6, 1–4.

Jove Jupiter, for the Romans the Lord of Heaven, appeared to Europa in the form of a beautiful white bull. When she mounted on his back he carried her off to Crete. She bore him a number of sons.

It is easier for a camel ... heaven Matthew 19, 24.

Giotto Giotto di Bondone (1267–1337) was an Italian painter, sculptor and architect.

Fra Angelico See note on Chapter 6.

Filippo Lippi Fra Filippo Lippi (1406–69) was an Italian painter.

Raphael Raphael Sanzio (1483–1520) was an Italian painter, regarded as one of the greatest artists of all time.

Magi The three wise men from the East who brought offerings to the infant Christ.

mystery play See note on Chapter 5.

Ascension The ascent of Christ which took place forty days after the Resurrection.

Touch me not ... father John 20, 17.

Rabboni ... John 20, 16. The word means teacher.

The Resurrection ... death This sentence and the following paragraph represent an important statement of Lawrence's attitude: his affirmation of life and the salvation in and through the body.

Revision questions on chapters 6–10

1 How far does the visit to Lincoln Cathedral symbolize the relationship between Will and Anna?

2 What does the honeymoon reveal about the characters of Will and Anna?

3 How far is it correct to say that Anna is a stronger and more dominating personality than Will?

4 Describe the relationship in these chapters between Will and Ursula.

Chapter 11

As she matures Ursula becomes aware of her own individuality. She tests the truth of religion by its reference to her daily life. She feels the conflict between the precepts of the Gospels and what she wants. She does not want to give all away because she hates the idea of being poor. Her need for Christ is sensuous, physical. Then along comes the young Anton Skrebensky. Ursula is sixteen. He is on leave from the Army where he is an engineer. She is fascinated by him, by his aristocratic self-sufficiency. They go about together, on walks and to the fair. She becomes increasingly aware of his physical presence; they begin to explore the world of love. Kissing becomes a language to them, as does the closeness of their bodies pressed against each other. His languor and indifference at once irritate and attract her. They play with love madly and dangerously. In the car in which he met her from school, his blood burns in him and Ursula is in ecstasy. Skrebensky returns for Fred's wedding. Ursula attacks him for being a soldier and for his own weak sense of identity. On a walk before the wedding party Ursula meets a couple on a barge; when they decide to call their previously nameless baby after her, Ursula gives her necklace to the baby. Later, at the wedding party she dances with Skrebensky. During the dance she is aware of the full moon outside; she is separate from him. His will wants to subdue her. After the dances they go to the stackyard. He feels destroyed in her kiss there; she annihilates him. As she returns to her normal self from her mood of destruction, she tries to restore him, to wipe out the memory of what has happened. He is glad to leave, to go about his duties, to think of the community rather than personal intimacy. Ursula is afraid of the nothingness that came over him. When they meet at the Marsh before he goes to the war in South Africa, they are as two strangers. Ursula's emotions and sexual life turn sour inside her.

The early part of this chapter reflects the constant self-questioning in Ursula. Biblical imagery and rhythms accompany her thoughts and show her main concerns at this period. The sensual passion she has for Christ is vividly described. But with the arrival of Anton Skrebensky the continuum of physical passion which characterizes the novel is developed. Ursula becomes more fully aware of herself and her physical appearance through Skrebensky's words. Notice that the swing-boats which were employed so tellingly as an incident (and a symbol) with her father are used again here to indicate her rising passion for Skrebensky. The latter's sexual passion is intensively conveyed through his story of the 'perfect maniac' who has to go up to town to find a woman. The dangers of the Ursula–Skrebensky relationship have been indicated above, but the individual egoisms, the struggle to subdue, has been seen in the earlier relationship described in this novel. Strangely, the reaction to this love gives Ursula a feeling of independence and well-being. When Skrebensky returns for the wedding their discussion underlines the differences between them. The incident with the couple on the barge is also a pointer to the difference in the characters and attitudes of Ursula and Skrebensky. Ursula is capable of responding naturally and uninhibitedly to the situation, just as later she is to respond mystically to the experience of darkness and nature. But the passion between herself and Skrebensky reflects the Lawrentian view of conflict – often destructive conflict – between the sexes, as well as emphasizing the sway and movement of emotion and physicality. They arrive at this state when Skrebensky departs: ' "You will come back to me?" she re-iterated. "Yes," he said. And he meant it. But as one keeps an appointment, not as a man returning to his fulfilment.'

feeding of the five thousand Matthew 14, 21.
the pillar of cloud across the desert Numbers 9, 15-21.
the bush that crackled Yet another reference to the burning bush.

Sell all ... poor Matthew 19, 21; Mark 10, 23.

And she went away ... clean This is reminiscent of the ideas of William Blake, to whom Lawrence has often been compared.

Oh Jerusalem ... would not Matthew 23, 37

Come unto me ... rest Matthew 11, 28–30.

Adam ... place i.e. the Garden of Eden.

three angels ... doorway Genesis 18.

perpetuum mobile Italian for perpetual motion, the term applied to some theoretical force that will drive a machine for ever.

Wuthering Heights A novel by Emily Brontë (1818–48), a wild love story of passion beyond death.

surged in a voluptuous ... way cf. Anna with Tom Brangwen.

grand dame Great lady (French).

laisser-aller Carelessness (French).

cynical Bacchus ... picture Probably a reference to the Young Bacchus painted by Michelangelo Merisi da Caravaggio (1573–1610). Bacchus is the Roman god of wine and jollity.

morris dancing An English folk-dance, usually danced by six men.

Creole A native of South America, the West Indies etc., with a European ancestor.

Mahdi The title of the messiah expected by Moslems; in particular assumed by the Sudanese leader Mohammed Ahmed, who besieged General Gordon in Khartoum. He was later defeated by Lord Kitchener.

Saint Ursula A British virgin saint reputed to have been murdered by the Huns in the Rhineland.

a pillar of salt The story of Lot. 'But his wife looked back from behind him, and she became a pillar of salt.' Genesis 19, 26.

And God blessed Noah ... destroy all flesh Genesis 9, 1–15.

dryads Wood nymphs.

fauns Rustic deities with horns, goat's feet, tail and pointed ears (Roman).

nymphs Female guardian spirits living in a tree, river etc.

Naiads Nymphs of lake or river (Roman).

Shem and Ham and Japheth Three sons of Noah.

God kissing carrion 'For if the sun breed maggots in a dead dog, being a God (or good) kissing carrion.' Shakespeare's *Hamlet*, Act II Scene 2.

War ... South Africa The South African or Boer War started in 1899 and finished in 1902. The Boers, the descendants of the

Dutch farmers who had settled there, fought against the British. The war began very badly for the British.
angel before Balaam Numbers 22, 22–3.

Chapter 12

Ursula is coming to the end of her schooldays. She knows she needs a matriculation qualification if she is to be independent in later life. But she finds much of the work tedious. Gudrun, who has discovered a gift for drawing, is a great comfort to her. Ursula conceives an admiration for one of the mistresses, Miss Winifred Inger. The relationship ripens into intimacy after they have been swimming together in the night, naked. Ursula learns a lot from her about religion and the Women's Movement. Ursula invites Winifred up to Yorkshire to meet Tom Brangwen, who works and lives in a squalid mining town that depresses Ursula utterly. Ursula is nauseated by Winifred's love for her, and relieved when Winifred and Tom plan to marry. Ursula has outgrown her love for both of them. Brangwen cares little for marriage but he wants children.

This is a further stage in Ursula's progression towards maturity. The relationship with Winifred Inger is convincingly described and developed through the swimming incident. Again we are aware of Ursula's capacity for physical and emotional experience, but also of her withdrawal into herself afterwards. Lawrence uses deliberate Biblical imagery to stress Ursula's nature – 'Her God was not mild and gentle, neither Lamb nor Dove. He was the lion and the eagle'. Winifred contributes to Ursula's education in the broadest possible sense, but knows when the moment of rejection has come. The introduction of Tom Brangwen into the narrative carries with it plenty of social and moral comment on 'the pit owns the man' theme. There is some cynical irony about Tom and Winifred coming together, their worship of the machine which Ursula cannot accept. As Lawrence puts it, her visit to Wiggiston effectively makes Ursula grow up.

As You Like It Shakespeare's comic play.
farouche Awkward (French).
Newnham A ladies' college at Cambridge.
Apollo Greek god of music and poetry, represented as a model of manly beauty.
A royal prince Gautama, the Buddha, was originally Prince Siddhartha or Gautama before he became the founder of Buddhism.
Osiris One of the chief gods of Egyptian mythology, judge of the dead, the creator, and the god of the River Nile.
Moloch God of the Ammonites to whom children were burnt in sacrifice. The word is now applied to any power that demands the sacrifice of what is dearest to us.
Women's Movement This was concerned with the fight for the vote and for women's equality.
Zolaesque Emile Zola (1840–1902) was a French novelist who practised his naturalistic theories by writing a series of novels which contained revolting descriptions of misery and vice.
vogue la galère 'Let the galley sail', a phrase meaning, 'Let's chance it', (French).

Chapter 13

After passing her matriculation examination, Ursula is not happy merely to remain at home hoping for marriage. Anna is having her ninth child, and her fulfilment in her breeding enrages Ursula. She is advised by her former headmistress to become an uncertified teacher and to take a degree at a training college. Her mother and father are hostile to the idea, although they do not actually forbid her to go ahead. When she obtains an interview in Kingston, her father manages to get her a post locally in a school in Ilkeston. At first she hates it. All her ideals of teaching are destroyed by the unruly class. Mr Harby, the headteacher, is a bully and hates her for her lack of discipline. The school is a prison to her. Yet she is determined that she will not fail in this man's world. She ceases to look at the children as individuals; instead she tries to exert her will over them. After she has fought and thrashed one particularly objectionable boy, Williams, she gains a measure of control although her results are poor. In Maggie Schofield, a fellow-teacher, she finds a friend and a consolation. Ursula believes in joy and lasting love whilst Maggie believes in suffering and change. It is this difference of outlook that finishes the friendship.

There is little doubt that this chapter derives in part from Lawrence's experiences in teaching before he became a full-time writer. The crowdedness of her domestic life oppresses Ursula, and she wishes to break out of it. Her father develops his creative impulses, while Ursula lives in her memories, seeing her younger self as dead. The conflict with her father typifies both their personalities. His possessiveness is revealed once more, and his getting her the local job shows his fear of losing her. The whole school experience serves to shatter Ursula's dreams, though it also shows her resilience as she survives Mr Harby, the children (particularly Williams) and Mrs Williams. Lawrence is bitter about what passes for education, the ritual rote learning which has nothing to do with understanding, the atmosphere, the moral blackmail. The Williams' episode is Ursula's coming of age, but attendant upon it is the self-degradation of having been forced to use violence. In Lawrence's words, 'It seemed as if a great flame had gone through her and burnt her sensitive tissue'. She is reduced to behaving mechanically in school. She grows away from Maggie because she refuses to be confined emotionally.

Donatello Donatello (1386–1466) was an Italian sculptor who revived the classical style and had a deep influence in the development of the Italian Renaissance.

Della Robbia A family of Florentine artists and sculptors.

Benvenuto Cellini Benvenuto Cellini (1500–71) was an Italian artist, silversmith and sculptor. He led an adventurous life, although perhaps not quite as exciting as described in his *Autobiography*.

training colleges For training teachers. Lawrence himself had followed the same route to a teaching qualification as Ursula takes.

Queen Anne House A house built in the style fashionable in the time of Queen Anne (1665–1714), characterized by the plain brick frontage, conformity of size and height, and pedimented doorways.

Richmond ... Queen Elizabeth As the Thames was the main thoroughfare in London at that time palaces were built on its banks. Well-known ones were Hampton Court (which still exists) and at Richmond.

Sweet Thames ... song From *Prothalamion* by Edmund Spenser (1552–99).

C'est la mère Michel ... rendra 'It is mother Michel who lost her cat who yells out of the window, who will bring it back to her.' French traditional children's song.

Greuze Jean Baptiste Greuze (1725–1805) was a French painter, one of whose best-known works is 'Innocence'.

Reynolds Sir Joshua Reynolds (1723–92) was a British artist who became the best-known portrait painter in the eighteenth century.

Board of Education Now known as the Department of Education and Science.

suffragette A member of the movement to gain votes for women.

She shall ... springs From a poem by William Wordsworth (1770–1850) – the last of the four 'Lucy' poems.

Why shall the children ... teach them cf. Lawrence's poem:
I am sick and what on earth is the good of it all?
What good to them or to me, I cannot see!

Chapter 14

Ursula visits the Schofields who live in a cottage behind Belcote Hall. Anthony, Maggie's brother, is much taken by Ursula. Maggie is hurt by Ursula's neglect. Something in Anthony appeals to Ursula; but when he proposes marriage she knows she cannot settle and she refuses him. The end of her days at school are rapidly approaching. Her father has been appointed a handwork instructor at the Grammar School in Willey Green. He buys with Anna's money quite a big house in the new part of Beldover. The last day of school brings a sense of freedom and exultation to Ursula. When she is presented with two books by Mr Harby she is moved and decides she likes her fellow-teachers. After all she has fought and won her battle there. The family is excited to be moving; they are all determined to enjoy their new house in full privacy.

This is a further register of change in Ursula. Her visits to Maggie's home show her the power she can exert over men. There is some pathos though in her rejection of Anthony – 'She could not help it, that she was a traveller'. With her father's promotion and increased status Ursula naturally feels that she is coming into her own, but first there is her leaving the school, the last ceremonies finding her quite moved despite herself. One of the best sequences in the novel has Lawrence successfully conveying the atmosphere of the move and the unfamiliarity of waking up in a new house.

Coleridge's *Christabel* Samuel Taylor Coleridge (1772–1834) was a romantic poet, critic and philosopher. *Christabel* is an unfinished poem, has a medieval setting and is about Christabel's meeting with a lady in distress who turns out to be a supernatural evil creature.

Botticelli Sandro Botticelli (1444–1510) was a Florentine painter who brought humanity to the treatment of religious subjects. His most famous picture is the 'Birth of Venus'.

Primavera A painting by Botticelli for the villa of the younger Lorenzo at Castello. It is now in the Uffizi Gallery. In it Venus welcomes the approach of spring.

Aphrodite The Greek goddess of love.

Swinburne's poetry Algernon Charles Swinburne (1837–1909) was a master of melodious verse who often shocked by his unconventional approach and paganism.

Meredith's George Meredith (1828–1909) was a poet and novelist. His best-known poem is *Modern Love*.

Chapter 15

They settle into the new house. In October Ursula is going to college. Gudrun is attending the Art School at Nottingham.

At first Ursula approaches her studies and the institution with reverence. She spends the holiday in Scarborough then goes to visit Tom Brangwen and his wife who now has a baby. During the next year at college Ursula becomes disillusioned in the place, her teachers and her studies. She concentrates on biology. Just before Easter she hears again from Skrebensky. He is coming to England for a few months before going to India. She looks forward to meeting him. He has become a man, sure of himself. She hates the position of superiority and authority that he will take up in India. Yet she loves him. They are very close during the walk at Trent Bridge on the first night. He possesses her finally during an evening walk near Beldover. She feels she has added another dimension to her everyday self. Skrebensky suggests marriage, but they see marriage as an entry into the ordinary world and a retreat from their own intense secret world. At Easter they stay in a hotel in Piccadilly where, remote in their room from the outside world, they pursue their relationship, which for them is the only reality. Then they go to Paris. In Rouen, on the way home, the first shadow descends on their relationship. Without her in London he feels he has ceased to exist. He writes to Ursula to urge marriage. They spend a few days in a country house near Oxford. Ursula is aware of the bliss of her own company when he is not with her. She owns and enjoys his body; he has become afraid of hers. Ursula attacks democracy, Skrebensky and his attitudes. She maintains he no longer satisfies her; he hates her. In Sussex Ursula can make love only on the downs, not in a house, not on a bed. When Ursula has to take her examination in London she will not stay with him. She refuses to marry him – ever. He is completely broken and weeps uncontrollably. They spend the night in an Italian hotel. Ursula feels separate from him. She is torn between marriage and teaching. They go as one of a large party to a bungalow on the Lincolnshire coast. They make love under the moon. Ursula feels cold and dead towards him; Skrebensky feels annihilated. The next morning they are strangers; it is over. He marries the daughter of his Colonel and sails to India with his wife.

Most of the important notation to this chapter is given in the summary above, but we notice that Ursula reduces Skrebensky, unmans him, and that their relationship is described by Lawrence with a terrible destructive intensity. Again, her college experiences cause her some loss of idealism. Her wish for freedom is seen in her reaction to the beauties of the sea. The intensity with Skrebensky only makes her the more aware of her self-freedom – or rather the need for it. Lawrence does convey in fact their dual independence of the world in their room in London – 'They alone inhabited the world of reality. All the rest lived on a lower sphere'. The simple explanation of Ursula's rejection is her need to have her own identity, not to be submerged, but to be alone. The staying on the downs, the complete freedom from convention, Ursula's mystic communication with nature, all this really excludes Skrebensky, even when he makes love to her. But Ursula is bewildered and made unsure by her own difference from others, and this leads to her nearly succumbing and marrying Skrebensky. There is a genuine pathos conveyed by her confusion. But she cannot hold to her decision to marry Skrebensky, and retains her individuality at the expense of his destruction. As noted above, he quickly marries his Colonel's daughter: it is the natural reflex of a man who has lost all security because of a relationship he didn't understand.

the Castle Nottingham Castle.

Racine Jean Racine (1639–99) was the greatest of the French tragic dramatists.

Livy Titus Livius (59 BC–AD 17) was a Roman historian.

Horace Quintus Horatius Flaccus (65–8 BC) was a Roman poet. He wrote *Satires, Odes* and *Ars Poetica*.

Cassandra Cassandra was the daughter of Priam, King of Troy. She had the gift of prophecy but no one believed her predictions.

Chaucer Geoffrey Chaucer (1340?–1400) is the first 'modern' English poet. His most famous work is *The Canterbury Tales*. His 'naiveté' is only in the appearance of the language and not in intention, style or artistic approach.

Beowulf An English poem that has an epic quality in its style and story.

unicellular One-celled organism (plant or animal).

ciliary Beating movement of fine 'hairs', like the movement of a field of corn as the wind blows over it.

nucleus Control centre or cell organizer and regulator.

nodalized Knotted.

Invisible Man The subject of a novel by H. G. Wells (1866–1946).

museau 'Animal face', snout, (French). It can also be used as a term of affection, 'pretty little face'.

Gewiss ... Baronin 'Certainly, Baron. You're welcome, Baroness' (German).

Chapter 16

Ursula goes to Beldover, shut up within herself. She tells the family that there will be no marriage with Skrebensky.

She thinks she is pregnant. She sends a letter to Skrebensky announcing her pregnancy, her sense of guilt in destroying their relationship, and her willingness to marry him. On an evening walk Ursula has a delirious nightmarish experience of being pursued by a group of horses. When she at last arrives home she goes to bed and is very ill for two weeks. She struggles in her illness to be free of Skrebensky and of any ties to people or to things. Then slowly she begins to sleep. When she wakes it is to a new dawn. Her experience with Skrebensky seems a distant memory. She is not pregnant. A cablegram from Skrebensky announces his marriage. A contempt for him grows in her. As she recovers she looks for a new creation but she is sometimes overwhelmed by the emptiness and futility of the people and things that she sees. Then she sees the rainbow linking the new houses to the top of heaven. The rainbow is a symbol of the new architecture based on Truth and destroying the ugliness of the houses and factories.

There is a fine combination here of the factual and the symbolic as Ursula comes through her ordeal and into a new and living and positive identity. There is a terrible irony in the letter to Skrebensky – in how hard Ursula tries to conform, and in her feeling sure of him who is already lost to her. The experience with the horses is cathartic – she is in a state of heightened imagination and fear anyway – and the sleep is not the sleep of death but of recreated life. She appropriates the mystical truth through the vision of the rainbow which links her earthly and spiritual life. A simple explanation of this is impossible. It is unique to the individual.

Revision questions on chapters 11–16

1 What contribution does Winifred Inger make to Ursula's development?

2 Describe the differences in Ursula's and Anton Skrebensky's attitude to society

3 Why is it important for Ursula to succeed in teaching? Show how this success is gained.

4 What part is played in *The Rainbow* by the younger Tom Brangwen?

The characters

Tom Brangwen

Things had puzzled him very much, so he had taken the line of easy, good-humoured acceptance.

Tom is the first of the three generations of Brangwens who form the subject of *The Rainbow*. He is the simplest and least complicated of them, perhaps because he is the least intelligent. In Lawrence's world the inability to think analytically and intellectually is one of the keys to happiness. He also lives in a simpler society, close to the land and relatively untroubled by the machine.

Tom is the youngest child, brought up with his sisters rather than with his brothers. At his grammar school in Derby, he fails to distinguish himself in any way. He is a sensitive youth, responsive to sensuous influences and to the emotional appeal of literature. His generous open nature is respected and he has one firm and deep friendship.

He is glad to finish with school and to begin work on the farm. He enjoys his life there and welcomes every experience. Sometimes he drinks too much with his companions. On one of these occasions, when he is nineteen, he goes with a prostitute; the experience is a shock to him and his ideas of womanhood. In his own home women have symbolized high moral attitudes, sensitivity, and secure social standards.

He is left completely responsible for the farm when his father is killed in an accident; Tom is seventeen when this happens. His mother dies when he is twenty-three.

His nature changes; his former eager cheerfulness changes to moods of black anger. He wants a woman, but he can forge no deep relationship with the good women he meets; casual affairs leave him dissatisfied and unfulfilled. He tries to lighten the intensity of his need by an increasing dependence on drink.

Tom is fascinated by the strange and the unusual in people. This finds expression in his interest in the foreigner, whether in the man whose mistress he has just possessed, or in Lydia Lensky whom he is to marry.

Lydia and her daughter Anna are the salvation of Tom Brangwen; they give to his life a meaning, a centre and a fulfilment. Lydia is quickly attracted to this handsome, fair-haired, blue-eyed man, full of strength, energy and health.

Tom feels inferior to his wife at the beginning, inferior in social position and to the brilliance of her dead husband. He is six years younger than she. Yet together they forge a relationship that is magnificently successful. He lives by, through and in her. There are times when he is jealous of her past and when he feels separate from her. When she is pregnant, he feels shut out. But always he knows that he needs her. His marriage is a significant achievement, although limited by his own nature and by a narrowness of expectation, compared to Ursula's demands on a relationship and marriage.

Tom works determinedly to establish a relationship between himself and Anna. It is hard work. The relationship is finally established when Lydia is in labour. He takes Anna everywhere with him, even to the cattle market. They are physically close. Anna loves to feel the nearness of Tom's large vital body as they ride in the gig together. Tom's love for Anna is an important part of his life, subsidiary to his love for Lydia but flowing from it. They sing nursery rhymes together; they are noisy and boisterous.

Tom's imaginative insight and understanding of even those closest to him are limited, in spite of his kindness, his generosity and his goodwill.

After the visit to his brother's mistress he realizes with a shock that he has failed to understand that his wife may feel lonely and insecure. When he does his love for her is deepened in understanding and in desire. There begins, after two years of marriage, a perpetual miracle. He is more than ever absorbed in his wife and the wonder of their love together – and in Anna.

As he grows older, he becomes stout. He lives his own satisfying life, caring little for his neighbours. He likes people, but he does not want intimacy with them. They respect him; he is generous to them. He cares little for the deeper meaning of things. When Anna tries to discuss people, he does not like it.

The courtship of Will and Anna causes the darker feelings to surface in Tom that have not been evident since before his marriage. His jealousy for Anna which has always existed leads him to feel rejected, old and finished. He is overwhelmed by her rejection of his fatherhood to her for he has cherished her calling him 'Father – Daddy'. His whole life seems to be empty. His only consolation lies in his long successful relationship with his wife. Yet his generosity triumphs, and he enjoys his role as the fairy godfather.

The marriage of Will and Anna shows up all the essential qualities of his character – his shyness in the church, his need for his wife's support and, above all, his inspired hymn of praise to marriage.

As Tom grows older, he develops into a gentleman farmer. He has two sons; the younger, Fred, is very like himself and takes over the routine management of the farm. Tom is reasonably well-off, willing to face life with a large and generous acceptance, conscious that, though there is much in life that was a mystery to him, he is not responsible for the world and its ways.

His death is perhaps typical of his life. In spite of its suddenness and its violence, it comes easily to him after an enjoyable evening in Nottingham and he is not wholly conscious of what is happening. As he drowns, he is cheerful yet puzzled. His wife, in her eerie crying out for him, symbolizes the closeness of their relationship.

Lydia Brangwen

She was curiously self-sufficient and did not say very much.

Lydia brings the outside world to the Brangwen family. She is responsible for the quirks and the obstinate individuality of the following generations.

When Tom Brangwen first sees her she is dressed in black and looks rather small and slight. She walks as if she does not wish to be noticed. Her face is pale, her eyebrows are thick and dark, and she has a wide mouth. She speaks English with a foreign accent that reveals her Polish background. She is a landowner's daughter, although her father had been deeply in debt. Her mother was German.

She had married when quite young Paul Lensky, a young doctor, a patriot and an intellectual. She had been swept along and utterly dominated by her husband. They had two children, who died, and then later Anna. She was his slave, his girl-bride, his admirer and unquestioning follower. For him she had little meaning or significance. His heart was in his ideas. The failure of the rebellion broke Paul Lensky. He died in London to which they had fled. Lydia felt he had never lived, never received what she had to give, never really known her.

Almost immediately she responds in her body to Tom Brangwen; he is the man to awaken her from the long stupor into which she had fallen after her husband's death. Yet Tom finds her strangely self-sufficient. She is very quiet even though her grey eyes shine mysteriously. When a son is born to them, Lydia begins to live more in the present. The memory of her former life recedes. Some of the separateness that has troubled Tom disappears. She becomes more English. Yet some of her early spirit and energy have gone too. Even the baby she loves from a distance, quite unlike the love Anna is to show to her babies. It is as if a barrier exists not only between her and the world but between her and those closest to her. When her two sons are growing up she does not worry about them fighting, so long as they are not near her. If she is concerned, she becomes angry and they fear her. Her approach to life remains fundamentally aristocratic. She does not care what her sons are accused of so long as they do not reveal themselves to be stupid or inferior.

Lydia, in spite of her apparent self-sufficiency, is the type of personality who arouses love in others and a desire to protect her. Even the little Anna has anxiety for her. Her relationship to her husband really comes into full glory when, after his visit to his brother's mistress, he realizes that deep down Lydia is lonely and uncertain. Up to that moment he has failed to satisfy her. He did not take her like a man as her first husband did. She complains that he ignored her or took her like an animal. After this discussion, they come together completely, after two years of marriage. She, like Tom, is born into another life. She is still separate; he still understands little of her foreign background; but they are vitally and meaningfully connected. They are one. Lydia represents for Tom the meaning and the purpose of life.

Lydia's own sense of separation from life around her is mirrored in the general isolation of the whole family at the Marsh. This is not a question of principle. She is shy yet courteous with visitors – but they make no impression on her. When they have gone, it is as though they have never existed. The Marsh is her kingdom; with her husband and her family she has everything that she wants. It is Lydia's surety and power within the family that angers Anna, and drives her to Tom. Even, however, when she is closest to him she is always aware of the strong dark connection that exists between him and her mother.

She had been brought up in the Roman Catholic Church. When her husband died she had been supported by the Church of England, and had nursed a dying vicar. The barrier that existed between her and the world is translated into her religion. She cares little for the forms of religion and any analytical approach is foreign to her. She accepts God as the source of all life, fearfully acknowledging His presence and His mystery.

She almost fears her sons because she can feel their problems and anxieties. Above all she wants peace and to be remote from life. She turns to her grandchildren and specially to Ursula for comfort and company. To Ursula she speaks of her past life and her two husbands. She exercises a deep influence over Ursula's maturing mind and emotions.

After the ninth chapter Lawrence seems to forget about Lydia. She has served her purpose in allowing him to develop the picture of the fulfilled relationship with Tom. She is dismissed finally, and almost accidentally, by a casual reference.

Anna Brangwen

She had the child, her palpable and immediate future was the child. If her soul had found no utterance, her womb had.

Anna is the central character in *The Rainbow*. Not only does she appear from almost the beginning to the end of the novel; she is also the link that brings together the other characters. and the different generations.

Anna was one year old when her father, Paul Lensky, died. She is four years old when Tom Brangwen first met her. Her three main relationships are fundamental to the novel – her relationships to Tom, to Will and to Ursula. Tom is the first of these. At first Anna is jealous of Tom, because she sees him as an intruder in her relationship to her mother. From the very beginning her spirit is evident – in her jealousy she tells Tom to leave her mother's bed. At this stage she rejects his tolerant overtures to her. She is a lively child, changeable, pre-occupied, imaginative yet not happy. Gradually the relationship between Tom and Anna grows. He loves Anna more than he loves his own son. Like his wife, she is a centre for his love. She goes everywhere with him. She specially loves going in the trap with him; sitting high up satisfies her desire for power and position. She has a wild arrogance; she dislikes people who acknowledge Tom and fail to speak to her. When she goes to the village school she shows a patronizing lack of respect towards the teacher. She has a strange scorn for ordinary people. Except for her mother and father she cares little for anybody. Her world is centred on herself; there is no room for intimacy with other people – not even her two brothers. The only person who makes a significant impression on her is her mother's friend, Baron Skrebensky.

As she grows she becomes tall and awkward. Her dark eyes lose their hostility. Her hair turns brown. At school in Nottingham she tries in vain to become a young lady. She turns against the world, and is comfortable only at home. Rebelliousness marks her attitude to school and to lessons. Her nature, impatient with petty restrictions and trivial details, forms an idea of pride and freedom. Alexandra, Princess of Wales, becomes one of her models.

She is critical even of those she loves; her father's drinking angers her. Her life becomes a source of frustration to her. The Church fails to satisfy her, as she finds the expression of her feeling in words hateful. Reading means little to her, and girl friends less.

At eighteen Anna meets William Brangwen, her cousin. At first he arouses a feeling of antagonism. His singing in church moves her to irrepressible laughter. Shortly, however, the two young people become interested in each other. Anna becomes more independent, even towards her mother and father. She is soon deeply and passionately in love with Will. They decide on marriage. Anna's strength of will and obstinacy of determination, perhaps also an unconscious movement towards her destined procreative life, are shown in her abrupt renunciation of her father when he opposes the marriage.

At her marriage, as well as revealing her slim ankle and small foot, she also shows her supreme confidence in herself, 'a vain white peacock of a bride'.

Anna triumphs in marriage. On her honeymoon at the cottage she gives herself up unreservedly to the sexual bliss and physical delights of the marriage bed. Will is troubled, but Anna revels in it. She glows with sensual delight, a quality Tom notices when he visits them: she overwhelms Will, scattering his ideas of order and propriety.

Yet, in spite of her physical delight in Will, his constant presence soon begins to irritate her. They begin to hate each other. Anna has a vivid consciousness of her own identity; Will's lack of it annoys her. His instinctive acceptance of life, relationships, and the church arouses her antagonism. She wants to know the meaning of things. This difference of attitude is most memorably summed up in their visit to Lincoln Cathedral, where Will opens himself completely and emotionally to the vast sweep of the cathedral, 'the perfect womb', 'the climax of eternity'. Anna feels something of his reaction, but she revolts against it. Her opportunity to destroy the whole spirit of his passionate feeling comes when she draws his attention to the carved sly little faces. 'She was spoiling his passionate intercourse with the cathedral.' It is Anna who triumphs. Her emphasis on fact has conquered his instinctual feeling. Anna is more complete than Will because she can both feel and think. She is in control of herself and her world. 'She had got free from the cathedral, she had even destroyed the passion he had.' Anna is violent in her refusal to be mastered by Will. She pushes away his tools when they are in her way. When he objects she will show no compunction. She does what she wants in small and large things, secure in the divine rightness of her own decision, attitudes and actions. She recognizes no authority over her. Sometimes she hates him and his ways; sometimes she loves him, needs him, and enjoys him; sometimes she accepts him; sometimes she rejects him; sometimes she is happy; sometimes she is miserable. In her conflict, there is an element of dissatisfaction. The simplicities of Tom Brangwen are not for her, yet he is right when he says to her in her misery, 'You love the man right enough ... That's all as counts.'

The key to Anna's happiness and subsequent fulfilment is in her pregnancy. It is perhaps significant of the battle between them that she cannot at first tell Will this supreme fact. Anna glorifies in her pregnancy. Will is afraid of her fulfilment as he feels separate and alone. Anna's supreme consummation is expressed in her dance. 'She danced in secret, and her soul rose in bliss. She danced in secret before the Creator, she took off her clothes and danced in the pride of her bigness.' (p.183.) This symbolizes the supreme, conquering Anna. She is not only fulfilled in herself; her husband is drawn into this rich world of fecundity which is to be the dominant force in Anna's future life. She is to have nine children altogether. Her house is to be a house of children, in which she will reign as the supreme mother. And her daughter Ursula will hate her for it. It is her fulfilment in child-bearing that enables her to resist the dark physical will of her husband, to make him serve her as an instrument of her fecundity.

The conflict is not over between them. She refuses to sleep with him. But when the baby is born, they recognize the limits of their relationship. He has learnt to be alone, although he always wants her. She needs his body. And soon she is pregnant again, caught in the cycle of birth and the blissful delight of feeding the child. This is sufficient for Anna. As child succeeds child she is absorbed in the delight of motherhood. She can still attack Will, for instance when he strikes Ursula after she has misbehaved in the church. They have evoked an unconscious formula that Anna's authority should be supreme by day and that she should belong to him at night. Their relationship is fully resolved after Anna has borne four girls. When Will comes home after meeting the girl in Nottingham, they find their real identity in each other, in the physical exploration and the excitement and satisfaction of which their bodies are capable. There is no tenderness, no gentleness, but passion overwhelms them, even to the exclusion of their feelings for the children.

In worldly things Anna is indifferent. Money, social position, friends are all matters of no importance to her. She is a dignified mother, cool, calm and secure in her relations with her children. Anna represents the immediate, real and ever-present sensation of life; religion has nothing to say to her. She is wholly concerned in the everyday things of life, in the care of a growing family, in the house, and a little local gossip. She goes about her work in a leisurely detached way. In one sense she is never quite personal and never a clearly identifiable individual. Ursula's attempts to develop her ideas are mocked by her mother with the 'cunning instinct of a breeding animal'. Anna is most absorbed in her children whilst they are babies.

Anna is forty before she awakes from her period of motherhood. This is symbolized in the move to a new house. Perhaps she is now ready to accept her relationship with her husband as the centre of her life. 'The silence of intimacy between the two made a home in the hearts of the children.' They want to be alone there; 'they wanted to do as they liked in their own home, with no stranger in the midst'.

William Brangwen

His real being lay in his dark emotional experience of the
Infinite, of the Absolute.

William is the son of Tom's brother Alfred, who has become a
draughtsman at a lace-factory in Nottingham, married a
chemist's daughter, and has a mistress.

William has black hair and reminds Anna of an animal that
lives in the darkness. He is tall and thin, shy yet strangely self-
possessed. He has a thin dark moustache. His eyes are golden-
brown, quick and steely like a hawk's. He has a good tenor
voice which he enjoys using. He is later to become choirmaster
of the local church.

His main interest is church architecture about which he
speaks passionately in spite of his usual hesitant speech. He is
an enthusiastic wood-carver. The first object he makes for
Anna is a butter stamper with a phoenix carved on it. During
his courtship he is working on a relief of the Creation of
Eve.

He hates his father, and loves his mother; yet his feelings
for them are paradoxically almost interchangeable. Tom
Brangwen thinks there is no core in him.

In Anna he arouses love. He himself is passionately in love
with her; he has a fierceness of purpose in his pursuit of Anna.
He wants her in marriage; he wants to possess her completely
for always. And he succeeds in spite of his poverty and her
father's opposition.

Will is worried by the complete withdrawal from the world
and the utter absorption in passion during the honeymoon. At
this time Anna is the more forceful character who sweeps
away his doubts, his standards and his preconceived ideas.
And he is glad to see them go. He is puzzled when, after this
experience of warmth and intensity, she suddenly becomes
irritated with him. She arouses all his anger, and his eyes burn
black and evil. He is like a beast of prey; Anna at these times is

afraid of him. Although he wants her desperately, in his anger he can repulse her advances. He fights with her. Their only contact is in their physical communion.

Will has an instinctual contact with ideas. He views the world through his emotions rather than with his mind. His religion is felt in his blood. He loves to dwell on the pictures in books of church paintings. He loves to give himself up to emotional exaltation as in the visit to Lincoln Cathedral. Anna hates this quality in him, and he hates her for her attempts to destroy his beliefs and upset his feelings.

His attempts to master Anna in the early days of their marriage are a notable failure. He can in no way modify or control her actions; she laughs at his attempts to do so. He wants to be the captain of the ship. When he tries to assert this position it bores her. Yet she is more afraid of his dark power and his insidious will to subdue her than he realizes. Anna compares unfavourably Will's dark intensity with her father's easy fresh lightness. Will is conscious that Anna does not respect him. She cares nothing about his work and his essential self; she is concerned only with him in relation to herself. He soon gives up 'the master-of-the-house idea'; he gives way to her. Through all their battles and their conflict, they still have their passionate love.

When Anna is pregnant Will fears his loneliness. Consequently he tries to force his will upon her; he is tense towards her; and she withdraws. He does not want her innocent love; it fails to satisfy him. In his unsatisfied, unfulfilled state he rages in constant anger. He resents Anna's fulfilment. He wants to be able to leave her, to become independent of her. He cannot; for him she is the only refuge. He can live only through her. And she hates his dependence on her. He is a man who has to have a woman – his woman. The problem he finds in his relationship to Anna is one he would have discovered in working out his relationship to any woman. He learns at last when she refuses to sleep with him not to force himself on her, but his need for her continues unabated. In the lessening of his demands on her they are able to become friends.

Will spends much time in the church; he looks after the stone and the woodwork with loving care. This is his main interest outside his family. He is not a man's man. He neither drinks nor smokes; he has no sense of self-importance. He cares little for the outer world of action or for his work. Home is the centre of his world and his real life. Work is merely an interruption to this.

From the moment of her birth he is drawn to Ursula; she arouses the strongest primitive love in him. He loves her to be near, enjoying the mere sensation of her presence. His love for her has its dark side, however, and sometimes he can hurt her by turning on her cruelly; this perverse streak is shown, for example, when he attempts to instil fear into her on the swings or in diving from the bridge. Ursula, on her side, is close to her father. When he is oppressed by the responsibility of being the father of four children, it is the presence of Ursula that supports him. His loneliness fascinates her.

His closeness to Anna is intensified by his night in the park with a girl. The strong force of his sexuality is shown by this incident. It is ironic that the result of his one attempt at unfaithfulness should be the permanent establishing of the right and ultimate relationship with his wife in the passionate mutual exploration of their bodies. He is overwhelmed by her 'Absolute Beauty', felt by his senses. This gives him a freedom in his life apart from her which he has never had before. He starts his night classes in woodwork when he is thirty – a step that is to lead later to his employment as a teacher and his release from work that has been meaningless to him.

Will Brangwen remains a powerful but shadowy character in the book. He is overwhelmed by Anna, and in the novel he exists to serve her. He has the right Lawrentian idea of the importance of male mastery, but he fails to achieve it. The admiration of author and reader goes to the Tom Brangwens who easily achieve consummation in their relationship. However, Will is closer to Lawrence than is Tom, and there is a lot of Lawrence in Will. He is not Lawrence, but he expresses much of Lawrence's dilemma in his own relationships and attitude to life. He is the precursor of those dark males whom Lawrence will create in *The Plumed Serpent* and some of the short stories. He is, however, a more successful and a more convincing creation than they are.

Ursula Brangwen

To be oneself was a supreme, gleaming triumph of infinity.

Ursula's is the most complex character study in *The Rainbow*. She is the most sensitively drawn character and she enshrines many of Lawrence's own feelings and ideas.

Her earliest connection with life is through her father. He awakes the consciousness in her that sets her apart from the other children. She has an intuitive understanding of her father, his personality and his problems that enable her to go on loving him even when he causes her pain. 'His life was based on her, even whilst she was a tiny child, on her support and her accord.' (p.220.)

Ursula's early capacity for sympathy can also be seen in her relationship with her widowed grandmother. It is to Ursula that she talks about her past life and her two husbands. From her Ursula receives her first intimations of what love between adults can mean.

Ursula finds being the eldest in a large family a great burden. Gudrun, her younger sister, has a great trust in her. Ursula feels that she can never be herself; she is submerged as the representative of the Brangwen family. She is proud, but she expects other people to like her. She does not scorn the children of poorer families; but she is disappointed when they fail to act according to her standards.

As Ursula grows older, she hates her mother's fecundity. She hates the lack of privacy in the house and the children's insistent demands for her attention.

At the Grammar School in Nottingham she is shy; she bites her nails. She has great expectations of her work there. She is quick and intelligent, but not systematic in her approach. Compulsion in learning is anathema to her, and leads to her hating teachers and lessons. In her rebellion she feels she is a law to herself. She tries to preserve the essential privacy of her individual self wherever she is. She loves Sundays because on that day she is free to be herself.

Ursula sympathizes with her father's mystical approach to religion. Jesus is for her another world, an escape from her everyday world of babies and domesticity. 'Ursula was all for the ultimate.'

As Ursula moves towards womanhood, she becomes more aware of herself. She loses her faith in the reality of religion, and begins to look upon the stories of that other world which has been so important to her as myths. She finds the moral precepts difficult. When her younger sister Theresa slaps her and she turns the other cheek which Theresa also hits, she goes about in frustration until she has her revenge. Then she feels clean but unchristian. All has to be judged by its relevance to weekday life.

It is at this time that she first meets Skrebensky. She is not yet good-looking. She does not know how to carry herself. Her dark hair is tied behind; her yellow-brown eyes are vague; her skin is golden and warm. She is quickly attracted to Skrebensky, and excited by physical contact with him. Her idealism colours her ideas of love. 'I think it's right to make love in a cathedral,' she asserts (p.298). Her relationship with Skrebensky centres round the intimacies of kissing. She knows it is a dangerous game, but she enjoys the defiance of it. Her school friend to whom she confides her relationship is rather contemptuous of Ursula's actions. But she feels a glory in the relationship and in the memory of it when he has gone.

Ursula's strong individuality is expressed in her dislike of the State. She dislikes Skrebensky's concept of a nation; she angers him at a later stage of their relationship with her aristocratic dismissal of democracy. Ursula is determinedly romantic and opposed to the ordinariness of most people's lives and their houses.

Skrebensky as a representative of this world creates a deadness in her. When she kisses him at the wedding party she finds nothingness in him. She feels destructive and cruel, quite different from the kind person she wants to be in the everyday world. Skrebensky's pride is humbled by her. The pattern of their relationship is established, and, on a more intense level, is to be repeated in their later relationship.

On leaving school Ursula is determined that she will make her mark in the world of men. She is conscious at this time that she has no real self, nothing to give to people. She envies her sister Gudrun's indifference. Ursula is anxious about people's reaction to her, about whether they like her, and all the time she feels different from them. She is comfortable only in the world of nature.

One influence on her at this time is one of her mistresses, Winifred Inger, with whom she becomes intimate. In discussion with her Ursula resolves that human desire is the yardstick of truth and goodness. Ursula's is a much finer and more sensitive nature than that of Winifred. A relationship that begins as a schoolgirl's thrilling admiration ends in her rejection of a woman whom she has found to be gross.

Teaching for Ursula is a way to independence. 'You have an emotional nature,' her former headmistress writes to her, 'a quick natural response. If only you could learn patience and self-discipline, I do not see why you should not make a good teacher.' (p.358.) Her father is less encouraging. 'And what sort of a teacher do you think you'd make? You haven't the patience of a Jack-gnat with your own brothers and sisters, let alone with a class of children. And I thought you didn't like dirty, board-school brats.' (p.359.)

Ursula's determination reveals itself in the way she goes about applying for a post in spite of her parents' hostility. Her romanticism is revealed in the dreams she conjures up of herself in these posts.

Ursula's sensitive idealistic nature is shocked by her experience in teaching. The quality of her will and the stubbornness of her determination are shown in the way she is able to sacrifice her ideals to the pedestrian necessity of exerting her will over the class to gain discipline and to make them work. Her will to succeed and her refusal to be beaten are important traits in her character. In the harsh real world Ursula fights her battle and she conquers. Independence is not just a concept in her philosophy; it is something for which she is prepared to fight hard. 'But she had paid a great price out of her own soul, to do this. It seemed as if a great flame had gone through her and burnt her sensitive tissue.' (p.405.)

Ursula's approach to life is still joyous. She believes in joy, in happiness, in the unchanging nature of things.

She knows what she wants. She is able to reject Anthony Schofield's offer of marriage without hesitation. She has been excited by his attentions but thinks he looks ridiculous trying to impress her with his Sunday clothes. She knows she is 'a traveller on the face of the earth'.

Ursula's critical mind swiftly leads her into disillusionment with her studies at college. She begins with high hopes; she ends with a sense of frustration when she realizes that the college is merely a factory preparing students for qualifications that will be useful in a machine-dominated society. The Latin class is 'a sort of second-hand curio shop'. 'What good was Anglo-Saxon,' she asks herself, 'when one only learned it in order to answer examination questions, in order that one should have a higher commercial value later on?' In the end she gives up all subjects except biology, and finally fails her degree in that.

In this period, however, the second phase of her relationship with Skrebensky has taken place, with the same ultimate result as before. In her relationship she grows to final maturity. 'She was no mere Ursula Brangwen. She was Woman, she was the whole of Woman in the human order. All-containing, universal, how should she be limited to individuality?' (p.444.) As with her mother and father during their honeymoon at the cottage, the room in the Piccadilly hotel becomes the whole of reality and the outside world is excluded. But this reality does not last. In her rejection of Skrebensky she reduces him to a broken thing piteously weeping in a taxi driving round London. She seeks freedom in running naked on the downs. She cannot make love in a house, and finally she cannot give herself to him in warmth and passion at all. Ursula returns time and time again to nature as a consolation.

She rejects Skrebensky, but the effort of will in doing so breaks her for a time. But out of illness and fever, there emerges the full sense of her independence and freedom. 'I have no father nor mother nor lover. I have no allocated place in the world of things.' In *The Rainbow* is the promise of a new world finer and more beautiful than the world of ugly industrialization.

The final conclusion to Ursula's development is forced, and it leaves her in a vacuum which is unsatisfactory to the reader. There can, however, be no easy reconciliation, in terms of the world or her relationships, with a character of Ursula's complexity. The conclusion is right in terms of Ursula's development even if it be wrong artistically.

Anton Skrebensky

He aroused no fruitful fecundity in her. He seemed added up, finished. She knew him all around, not on any side did he lead into the unknown.

Anton Skrebensky is a minor character in the novel. He and his family appear in the book from time to time. They emphasize the foreign element in the Brangwens, that prevailing apartness which they hold in common.

He is the son of Baron Skrebensky, Lydia Brangwen's Polish friend, who had married a young English girl. Even as a young child he shows a cool lack of lasting interest when he comes in with his nurse to meet Anna and Will. He is Ursula's first love, but even in her limited girl's approach to physical passion she has realized his nothingness, and she has also attacked his unquestioning acceptance of the social order. So it is on the second phase of their acquaintance some years later.

There is love between them, and they explore fully the physical bounds of love. But it does not develop. Ursula feels in him and in his love a constriction of her freedom and sphere of activity. There is no depth in him, and she is finally conscious only of his nothingness. Perhaps it sums up his superficiality when he is able to turn from his relationship with Ursula almost immediately to marry the daughter of his colonel. The relationship between him and Ursula has indeed been a failure.

He is limited even in his love-making. He becomes afraid of Ursula's body. In spite of his wanting her, he feels a constraint, a fear. He cannot match Ursula's passionate intensity. 'Her whole soul was implicated with Skrebensky – not the young man of the world but the undifferentiated man he was.' (p.452.)

He has no real connection with society. He is a wanderer but not in the sense that Ursula is a wanderer on the face of the earth. He travels because, unlike the Brangwens, he has no real roots. In his travelling, however, he follows accepted social patterns whether it is in South Africa or in India. Skrebensky is always firmly a part of his class, his profession, his country and his society. He never challenges his place in them and accepts unquestioningly the given order of things.

Themes

Lawrence's only theme in *The Rainbow* is the exploration of the relationships between men and women. It is not the story of a family in the Victorian and Edwardian tradition. The fact that it deals with three generations of the Brangwen family is incidental to his use of each generation as an example of a different type of relationship. The development of the plot is the development of the theme.

In one sense, if we leave out marrying, giving in marriage, and considering the possibility of marriage, little happens. The incidents that remain in the memory are static incidents that crystallize a mood, an emotion or a situation between men and women. They are not part of an organic sequence of events.

The scene in Lincoln Cathedral is memorable, but only as a symbol of the conflict in the relationship between Will and Anna that existed before the scene and continues after it. Nothing is advanced; nothing is resolved by it. Anna's dancing naked when she is pregnant symbolizes her whole life given over completely to the rich fecundity of motherhood – at least to the age of forty and throughout the novel. The strength of the scene is in the power of the symbol and in the poetic presentation of the act itself, not in its revelation of Anna's character or in furthering any narrative intention.

There is a feeling of inevitability about the unfolding of events that largely removes the possibility of any narrative excitement. When Tom Brangwen is opposed to Anna's marriage to Will, there is no feeling that Anna's marriage is in jeopardy. Even in the powerful exchange when she rejects him as her real father, there is no sense in which this could be held to interrupt the inevitable unfolding of Anna's destiny as a richly procreative woman. It is significant only as a revelation of Tom's attitude and feelings to Anna and to his marriage.

Ursula's teaching experiences are an exception. The reader is concerned with whether she will fail or succeed, as well as with the impact of her experience on her ideas and her character.

Whether or not we regard *Women in Love* as a sequel, as Lawrence seemingly did, it is this lack of narrative that makes the ending of *The Rainbow* unimportant in terms of leaving the reader with a sense of completion. There can be no resolution because Ursula is only on the threshold of life. The first generation is resolved in the completion of death, or in Tom's death, for Lawrence gives scant attention to his wife after his death and her musings on her past life to Ursula. The second generation, Will and Anna, are resolved in so far as they have reached a working pattern in their relationship.

The reader might speculate on what will happen in the new house now that Anna's childbearing days are over. However, in terms of plot, it is possible to rest on the statement that 'the silence of intimacy between the two' made 'a home in the hearts of the children'.

The ending indeed points to a theory which may have been a major preoccupation with Lawrence when he was writing – the impact of the machine civilization on the quality of man's life. The wheel comes full circle when in the later *Lady Chatterley's Lover* Lawrence sees in the richness and significance of the sexual relationship an answer to the ugliness and purposelessness of industrial civilization. In spite of his preoccupation in *The Rainbow* with sexual relationships, his hope in the future is based on the vision of a new architecture, 'the old brittle corruption of houses and factories swept away, the world built up in a living fabric of Truth, fitting to the overarching heaven'.

This future is tackled far more seriously in *Women in Love*, where he was writing of contemporary England. In this sense

The Rainbow is a prelude, examining through a story of three generations, that is historically, the situation with which he was to deal in *Women in Love*.

Lawrence's novels were not based on a plot that was worked out in detail. He first of all conceived a work in his imagination. It was then written. This leads to the lack of inevitability in the development of the plot. One might question the accidental nature of Tom Brangwen's ending. The real point is that he had played his part in the development of the theme, and it was time for him to go.

When he began *The Sisters*, the title of an early version of *The Rainbow*, he probably had in mind a short novel, written in the first person. Ella Templeman, Ursula's prototype, was clearly based on Frieda Lawrence.

He sent another version called *The Wedding Ring* to Edward Garnett, his publisher's chief literary adviser, warning him that this work was very different from *Sons and Lovers*. Garnett was disappointed in the work; he found difficulty in sorting out the characters and described it as a sort of Russian novel written by George Eliot. Lawrence began the work again, for about the seventh time. He thought the earlier attempt was 'full of beautiful things – but it missed – I knew it just missed being itself'. It was Frieda's insistence that led to the title of *The Rainbow* being adopted. In some ways *The Wedding Ring* might have been a better title and certainly would have represented a better indication of the theme of the novel.

There can be no justification for the view that Lawrence was a swift writer, lacking in self-criticism. *The Rainbow* was rewritten many times, although some of these revisions or rewritings can be ascribed to not getting the right conception of the book sorted out in his mind before he began. Describing one revision, he wrote: 'This was the crude fermenting of the book. I'll make it into art now.' In the end Lawrence knew that his approach was right, and he refused to change it.

'Primarily,' he wrote, 'I am a passionately religious man, and my novels must be written from the depth of my religious experience. That I must keep to, because I can only work like that.' Certainly, in *The Rainbow* Lawrence expressed this feeling, but it was about sexual relationships that he felt 'passionately religious'.

When Lawrence changed to Methuen in publishing *The Rainbow* he rewrote the work yet again, making an eighth version.

The setting of *The Rainbow* is the Midlands in which Lawrence grew up. Cossethay is the village of Cossall; Cossall Church is the Cossethay Church that Will lovingly served; and Church Cottage, Cossall is the Yew Cottage of the novel. The parallels, the changes, the equivalents can be followed by those interested in attempting to trace the sources of a writer's imagination by literary detective work. In *The Rainbow* Lawrence views the world of the Midlands from a distance; he was wandering around Europe for much of the time whilst the novel was growing in his mind.

Astonishingly enough, in spite of its imaginative sweep, *The Rainbow* is a sensitive and accurate record of the social settings and attitudes of a small part of the English provincial scene. It also records through the three generations the development in social outlooks and the changing economic and industrial scene. It is very easy to forget how detailed this incidental background is and how many points of life it touches – education from infant to degree stage, industry and its development, family life in all its phases from childbirth through wedding parties to funerals. Unlike Jane Austen who makes no mention of the Napoleonic Wars, Lawrence not only mentions the South Africa War but discusses the whole question of war in some detail.

If there is a development in the theme, it is one of the increasing complexity of life, and the conditions in which life is lived and relationships are forged. The first generations quickly settle into their fulfilled married life. They accept their differences, yet rest on their essential unity. The conflict in the second generation is longer and more terrible. Ultimately they find a fulfilment, but it is more complex and perhaps less secure than that of the first generation. Finally Ursula fails to find fulfilment, partly through the nature of Skrebensky, partly through her own fierce independence and complex demands from relationships, and partly from the changed nature of a society dominated by industrialization, the machine, materialism, and the development of a changing role for woman in the home and in her relationships with men. Parallel to these main movements are occasional sidelong glances at other relationships, at Alfred with his mistress, at young Tom with Winifred. Again significantly in terms of development the second is far more complex than the first.

Style

The style of *The Rainbow* represents a revolutionary development both in terms of English literature and of Lawrence
himself. *The Rainbow* is a substantial stylistic advance on *Sons
and Lovers* in forging a style that was capable of expressing the
passionate depths and the subtle nuances in the relationships
of men and women. Lawrence himself said: 'I knew as I
revised the book, that it was a kind of working up to the dark
sensual or Dionysic or Aphrodisic ecstasy which does actually
burst the world, bursts the world-consciousness in every individual.' He talked about 'the new style' which he described as
'a hard violent style full of sensation and presentation'.

The prevailing feeling of the novel is the glory of life as
expressed in the flesh, and this is reflected in the style. From
the beginning this quality is emphasized in phrases such as
'the drowse of blood intimacy', 'pulsing heat of creation', 'the
pulse of the blood of the teats of the cows beat into the pulse of
the hands of the men'. These examples are all taken from the
first four pages of *The Rainbow*. There is a rise and fall in this
feeling; it is at its most intense in the chapters dealing with
Will and Anna Brangwen; it is least seen in the more complex
relationship between Ursula and Anton Skrebensky. Anna
herself is the consummation of this feature of the style.

The choice of word is always suggestive of life, vitality and
fruitfulness – even in the pains of childbirth. 'But to her it was
never deathly. Even the fierce, tearing pain was exhilarating.
She screamed and suffered, but was all the time curiously
alive and vital. She felt so powerfully alive and in the hands of
such a masterly force of life, that her bottom-most feeling was
one of exhilaration.' In this passage we have the emphasis on
'exhilarating' and 'exhilaration'; 'alive' is used twice, and
emphasized by 'curiously' and 'powerfully': with the denial of

death – 'vital' and 'masterly force' – the passage is a tremendous assertion of life and vitality.

The repetition, sometimes in the same form and sometimes in the form of a varied key word, is a very significant feature of the style. Such a word is 'fecund' which is abundantly used throughout. Ursula rejects Skrebensky because 'he aroused no fruitful fecundity in her'; 'fruitful' added repetitively to 'fecundity' increases its power. In the following lines the word is used four times:

... enveloped in the warm, fecund flow of his kiss, that travelled over her, flowed over her, covered her, flowed over the last fibre of her, so they were one stream, one dark fecundity, and she clung at the core of him, with her lips holding open the very bottom-most source of him.

So they stood in the utter, dark kiss, that triumphed over them both, subjected them, knitted them into one fecund nucleus of the fluid darkness.

It was bliss, it was the nucleolating of the fecund darkness.

It is not only the repetition of the idea of fecundity that is important here; there is also the direct repetition at the word 'flow', 'flowed', 'fluid', and the repetition of the idea. There is the almost wilful play on 'nucleus' and 'nucleolating'. Such a passage, and there are many like it, makes an assault on the reader's senses through its repetition, its rhythm, and the complete subordination of the idea to the creation of a sensuous appeal.

The basic problem of language in *The Rainbow* lies in its use to express the feeling and the meaning of sexual experience. Lawrence does not use the accepted although socially unacceptable words to describe sexual intercourse and lovemaking as he does in *Lady Chatterley's Lover*. Rather does he attempt to create the sensations of sexual desire and fulfilment or non-fulfilment by poetic and imaginative intensity of language. In this approach he enhances the beauty and the mystical nature of the sexual act and the emotions surrounding it. The use of religious images and reference is part of this approach. When Tom Brangwen contemplates his union with Lydia, he refers to his Gethsemane and his Triumphal Entry. God is regarded as having 'passed through the married pair'. When Anna declares her love, Will feels that 'the hand of the Hidden Almighty, burning bright, had thrust out of the darkness and gripped him'. The image of God burning in the bush is used on a number of significant occasions. It is appropriate that Ursula should think it is right to make love in a cathedral.

Yet it is repetition and rhythm that remain his most powerful stylistic devices in the description of sexual experience. This can be seen in the description of Will's making love to the girl in the park. 'He liked her – he liked the feel of her – he wanted to know her more closely. He let his fingers subtly seek out her cheek and neck. What amazing beauty and pleasure, in the dark.'

There is the rich abundant use of emotive words. 'There was no tenderness, no love between them any more, only the maddening, serious lust for discovery and the insatiable, exorbitant gratification in the sensual beauties of her body.' The contrast to the climactic emotional sweep often lies in the use of descriptive detail whether of scene or body. 'Tonight I shall know the little hollow under her ankle, where the blue vein crosses,' says Will. Tom's feelings for Lydia are revealed in 'her head, so shapely and poignant, that revealed her his woman to him'.

Words like 'completeness', 'connexion', 'womb', 'intimacy', 'consummation' are used to express the mysterious oneness of the sexual act. But the words can also be used outside the context of the actual act. This gives to the whole novel a brooding atmosphere of sex and procreation. When Will visits Lincoln Cathedral, 'he was to pass within to the perfect womb'. Sex is universalized by references to the moon. Ursula 'stood filled with the moon, offering herself. Her two breasts opened to make way for it'. Nature too plays a part. The woman's body is often likened to a flower. 'Her body opened wide like a quivering anemone.'

Darkness is repeatedly associated with the world of sexual activity. When Tom and Lydia reach their complete consummation after two years of marriage, it is 'received within the darkness which should swallow him and yield him up to himself. If he could come really within the blazing kernel of darkness ...' The darkness is often a symbol for undirected sexual desire: 'Waves of delirious darkness ran through her soul.' The idea can be more direct. 'He seemed like the living darkness upon her, she was in the embrace of the strong darkness.'

The dark is not always welcome. Anna rejoices in leaving the intensity and darkness of her husband for her father who is 'so fresh and free and all daylight'. The conflict between Will and Anna is summed up in the play on the idea of darkness. She goes to him radiant and innocent, but his reaction is summed up in 'dark spasm', 'dark' face, 'black' heart, 'black torment'. The final reconciliation is in terms of the light and the dark; she is mistress during the day and he is master in the dark of the night.

The idea of darkness is balanced by the idea of light, and there is an abundance of words and images suggesting light and warmth. Tom Brangwen is 'dimmed' by Lydia's departure. Her presence is 'as if a strong light were burning there'. 'The light of transfiguration burned on in their hearts', when they achieve their full consummation. Sometimes darkness and light are united. 'Here she would open her female flower like a flame, in this dimness that was more passionate than light', Ursula says when she meets Skrebensky in the church. Ursula for her father 'was a piece of light that really belonged to him, that played within his darkness'. The idea of warmth is closely connected with that of light, and is often equated with sexual fulfilment and satisfaction. So Tom finds Will and

Anna 'very glowing' when he visits them during their honeymoon.

Descriptive words are important. Sometimes they can be used for emphasis, sometimes for adding to the idea, sometimes to jolt the reader. Thus we get a 'great, scalding peace'. Words are often yoked strangely together, as in an 'anguish of thankfulness' or 'weeping hopefully'.

Some of the most felicitous passages in *The Rainbow* are concerned with nature and its description. The natural world is ever-present in the novel, not only as a setting but as a significant background that mirrors the moods and feelings of the characters. Life is often measured in terms of nature; the dying vicar was dead 'by the time the snowdrops were out'. To Lydia in her sorrow, nature is alive; she passes the gorse bushes, 'shrinking from their presence'. She steps into the heather 'as into a quickening bath that almost hurt'. Ursula, frustrated by the future of her relationship with Skrebensky, yearns for the open world of the downs; this symbolizes her own feelings, 'suffering only a few bushes to trespass on the intercourse between their great, unabatable body and the changeful body of the sky'.

Lawrence's keen and observant eye for nature is revealed in his descriptions, not only in the set-pieces but also in the incidental references. Thus Anna's happy ecstasy in her pregnancy is shown when she wanders out of doors 'where the catkins on the big hazel bushes at the end of the garden hung in their shaken, floating aureole, where little fumes like fire burst out from the black yew-trees ... the cowslips twinkled like manna, golden and evanescent on the meadows'.

Sometimes people are likened to animals in the description of their character. The man with the girl Tom meets in Matlock is likened to a monkey; Will Brangwen is compared to a hawk.

The style is generally marked by urgency and emotional intensity. One of the problems of such a style is that it can easily fall into excess and absurdity. And this sometimes happens in *The Rainbow*. It is a matter of total impression rather than particular passages. The poetic and imaginative are appropriate to the moments of heightened emotion. The difficulty is that much of *The Rainbow* is built up of such moments.

Sometimes the intensity is too prolonged, and the reader has a feeling of surfeit. The style is at times overwrought, especially in the attempts to describe the love between Ursula and Skrebensky. Perhaps the fault lies in the nature of the subject matter as much as in the style; the style is over-whelming when the subject matter is concerned with states of emotional intensity and sensual consciousness for too long.

It is this aspect of the style and subject matter that aroused hostility when *The Rainbow* was first published and still pro-vokes criticism from many readers. John Galsworthy, a con-temporary novelist and playwright, wrote that the 'perfervid futuristic style revolts me. Its reiterations bore me to death ... There is a spurious creativeness about it all, in spite of incred-ible assertions and pretence of sounding life to its core ... By dwelling on the sexual side of life so lovingly he falsifies all the values of his work – for this reason if for no other: the sexual instinct is so strong in all of us that any emphasis upon it drags the whole being of the reader away from seeing life steadily, truly and whole; drags it away from the rest of the book, stultifies the writer's own efforts at the presentation of human life and character.'

That is very much the Soames Forsyte in Galsworthy speaking, but it is a fair representation of what many people did and still do feel about Lawrence's style and subject matter.

What we must remember is that, although these qualities can be found in *The Rainbow*, they are often avoided. The world of inner conflict and emotion is frequently reflected in or shifted to the outer world by descriptions of scene, of people or of nature. This helps to externalize some of the subjectivity.

The usual division between thought and feeling is lacking in Lawrence; they are fused into one. Ideas are held with a passionate intensity by Lawrence and by his characters.

Ursula's quest for the ultimate, for truth and significance in religion, is of this kind. No one would expect Ursula to approach the expression of her ideas with a cold rationality or intellectuality. They are expressed clearly, meaningfully and powerfully, and that is appropriate to the character in this novel. To condemn Lawrence because he is not an intellectual novelist is not only nonsense; it is also irrelevant and reveals an ignorance of Lawrence's peculiar achievement and greatness. When the question of religion is considered it is through the eyes of a maturing girl and a young woman. The style and the presentation are appropriate to this. Nor is Lawrence the sort of novelist like Tolstoy who from time to time stands back from his characters in order to comment on them and their ideas and to develop his own. Lawrence has this astonishing power of identification with each of his main characters.

Fundamentally the writing represents a unity. People, background and actions are fused into one when they are described.

Ideas are presented through the exploration of the minds and attitudes of a variety of characters. This Lawrence does successfully. Ursula is balanced by Winifred Inger; Will by the younger Tom Brangwen and Skrebensky; the elder Tom Brangwen by Will; Anna by Ursula. Of course, Lawrence is not objective in his approach. His sympathies are wholly with Ursula and not with Winifred. But it would not be easy to say exactly where the novelist stands in the conflict between Will and Anna. It is not important, because Lawrence's characters are not always consistently and finely drawn. Sometimes in certain scenes they cease to be recognizable as clearly defined characters and become symbols of elemental states of joy, or fulfilment, or anger, or despair. Yet sometimes they can be remarkably and individually human, as Tom Brangwen is so often in his relationship to Anna, or in Will's remarks on Ursula's attitude to children when she announces her intention of becoming a teacher.

Lawrence's characters never become mere intellectualized puppets in his hands; he is too closely identified with them for that to happen. This identification has its own dangers, for in it the objective existence of a character can be submerged. 'You mustn't look in my novel for the old stable *ego* of the character,' Lawrence asserted. He is right, but the reader may complain that without stable and logically developed characterization, the plot and the theme as well as the characters can become confused. That, however, happens only occasionally in *The Rainbow*; but it does happen.

Lawrence's dialogue is expertly handled The natural spoken rhythms of English come through in the speech of his characters.

Lawrence's style can also be surprisingly effective in its approach to narrative. The accounts of Ursula's experiences in school reveal an economy of narrative style that carries the reader along. Connected with this is his gift for briefly delineating character. The mistress of Tom's brother Alfred plays only a very small part, yet she is described with a sureness of touch that gives a convincing picture, not only in terms of appearance but also in outlook and prevailing atmosphere. The same applies on a larger scale to Winifred Inger with whom Lawrence is manifestly not in sympathy. The bargee and his wife are wonderfully evoked, and even such a minor character as the taxi-driver who carries Ursula and the weeping Skrebensky to Hyde Park Corner remains distinct in the mind of the reader.

Lawrence can write plainly and succinctly when this is the right way to make an impact. 'Yes, they are pretty bad. The pits are very deep and hot, and in some places wet. The men die of consumption fairly often. But they earn good wages.' A novelist committed to naturalism could not write more simply and more powerfully than that.

The reader will almost certainly leave *The Rainbow* with an overwhelming impression of powerful emotional and imaginative writing. And that impression will be right. Closer analysis, however, reveals that Lawrence was a master of a variety of styles, even though in *The Rainbow* he is chiefly concerned with a language that is trying to express successfully the ecstasy, the misery and the conflict inherent in the deep relationships between men and women.

General questions and sample answer in note form

1 Compare the relationship between Tom and Lydia with that between Anton Skrebensky and Ursula.

2 *The Rainbow* replaces a plot by a series of significant incidents. Discuss.

3 Describe the main features of Lawrence's style.

4 'Its reiterations bore me to death. There is a spurious creativeness about it all.' How justified is this attack by John Galsworthy on Lawrence's style?

5 Lawrence excels in the vivid presentation of minor characters. Show, with examples, how far this is true.

6 Anna is the central and most important character in *The Rainbow*. Discuss.

7 Lawrence is closer to Ursula than to any other character in *The Rainbow*. Examine this statement.

8 What aspects of Lawrence's biography are important to the full understanding of *The Rainbow*?

9 The relationship between Tom and Lydia is the only one that is carried through to a conclusion. Discuss.

10 The ending of *The Rainbow* is artificial and unsatisfactory. Is this a justified criticism?

11 Choose any three aspects of the social background shown in *The Rainbow*. Describe their importance in the novel.

12 What do we learn about the importance of education in school from *The Rainbow*?

13 What impression is given of the quality and purpose of university education?

14 Which of the three major relationships is the most interesting?

15 *The Rainbow* is a great novel because it extends and deepens the reader's relationships between men and women. Discuss.

Suggested notes for essay answer to question 1

(a) *Introduction* (i) First Tom's nature and the meeting with Lydia – his appraisal of her – his fascination – his proposal – age and culture difference – his sense of closeness and separation – then Lydia's own earlier marriage and history – her nature and character.

(ii) Ursula – her nature and relationship with her father (and mother) – her meeting with Skrebensky – initial reactions – his inheritance and nature – first responses to her.

(b) The development of the Tom–Lydia relationship – physical communion – differences – growing apart her rejection of him – arrival of child *and* Tom's relationship with Anna. Coming together again – depth of love.

(c) Ursula – her childhood and development – then the coming together with Skrebensky: his languor and indifference and the effect on Ursula – the meeting with the couple on the barge (and the baby); Skrebensky wishes to subdue her – she 'annihilates' him; Ursula aware of change and sourness – the breaking of Skrebensky later.

(e) *Conclusion* – characters of Tom and Skrebensky different – physical communion similarities and differences – possession – self-destruction – passion – freedom; then Lydia – withdrawn – sense of apartness and strangeness – foreign – the child and the children – age. Ursula – how different from Lydia – factors which make her character – feelings – need for self expression. Sum up differences in couples clearly and with quotations, but indicate similarities briefly too.

Further reading

Works by D. H. Lawrence
Women in Love (Heinemann: Phoenix edition, and Penguin) is the obvious work to read after *The Rainbow*.

Sons and Lovers (Collins, Heinemann: Phoenix edition, Penguin) is worth reading on its own account; and it contains interesting points of comparison to *The Rainbow*.

Lady Chatterley's Lover (Heinemann: Phoenix edition) considers the themes of sexual fulfilment, and the industrial society.

The Woman Who Rose Away and other stories (Penguin) can also be read with profit and enjoyment. Lawrence's poetry should also be read for an insight into the author, as well as being enjoyable for its own sake. There are many selections available.

Books about Lawrence
D. H. Lawrence, Novelist by F. R. Leavis (Chatto & Windus) is the work of a critic who has consistently championed Lawrence.

Thought, Words and Creativity (Chatto & Windus), also by F. R. Leavis, contains a chapter on *The Rainbow*.

Son and Lover, P. Callow (The Bodley Head), covers the earlier part of Lawrence's life, including the period of his writing *The Rainbow*.

D. H. Lawrence, H. T. Moore (Heinemann: Phoenix) covers the author's entire life.

D. H. Lawrence, The Critical Heritage, edited by R. P. Draper (Routledge and Kegan Paul), contains a selection of contemporary reviews of *The Rainbow*.

This is but a small selection from the many books on Lawrence. The reader must, to a large extent, make his choice in terms of availability and interest in different facets of Lawrence's life, art and ideas. *The Cambridge Bibliography of English Literature* gives a comprehensive list.

Brodie's Notes

TITLES IN THE SERIES

Edward Albee	**Who's Afraid of Virginia Woolf?**
Jane Austen	**Emma**
Jane Austen	**Mansfield Park**
Jane Austen	**Pride and Prejudice**
Samuel Beckett	**Waiting for Godot**
William Blake	**Songs of Innocence and Experience**
Robert Bolt	**A Man for All Seasons**
Charlotte Brontë	**Jane Eyre**
Emily Brontë	**Wuthering Heights**
Geoffrey Chaucer	**The Franklin's Tale**
Geoffrey Chaucer	**The Knight's Tale**
Geoffrey Chaucer	**The Miller's Tale**
Geoffrey Chaucer	**The Nun's Priest's Tale**
Geoffrey Chaucer	**The Pardoner's Prologue and Tale**
Geoffrey Chaucer	**Prologue to the Canterbury Tales**
Geoffrey Chaucer	**The Wife of Bath's Tale**
Wilkie Collins	**Woman in White**
Joseph Conrad	**Heart of Darkness**
Charles Dickens	**Great Expectations**
Charles Dickens	**Hard Times**
Charles Dickens	**Oliver Twist**
Charles Dickens	**A Tale of Two Cities**
Gerald Durrell	**My Family and Other Animals**
George Eliot	**Silas Marner**
T. S. Eliot	**Selected Poems**
Henry Fielding	**Tom Jones**
F. Scott Fitzgerald	**The Great Gatsby** and **Tender is the Night**
E. M. Forster	**Howard's End**
E. M. Forster	**A Passage to India**
John Fowles	**The French Lieutenant's Woman**
Anne Frank	**The Diary of Anne Frank**
Mrs Gaskell	**North and South**
William Golding	**Lord of the Flies**
Graham Greene	**Brighton Rock**
Graham Greene	**The Power and the Glory**
Graham Handley (ed)	**The Metaphysical Poets: John Donne to Henry Vaughan**
Thomas Hardy	**Far From the Madding Crowd**
Thomas Hardy	**The Mayor of Casterbridge**
Thomas Hardy	**The Return of the Native**
Thomas Hardy	**Tess of the D'Urbervilles**
L. P. Hartley	**The Go-Between**
Aldous Huxley	**Brave New World**
James Joyce	**Portrait of the Artist as a Young Man**
John Keats	**Selected Poems and Letters of John Keats**
Philip Larkin	**Selected Poems of Philip Larkin**

D. H. Lawrence	The Rainbow
D. H. Lawrence	Sons and Lovers
D. H. Lawrence	Women in Love
Harper Lee	To Kill a Mockingbird
Laurie Lee	Cider with Rosie
Christopher Marlowe	Dr Faustus
Arthur Miller	The Crucible
Arthur Miller	Death of a Salesman
John Milton	Paradise Lost
Robert C. O'Brien	Z for Zachariah
Sean O'Casey	Juno and the Paycock
George Orwell	Animal Farm
George Orwell	1984
J. B. Priestley	An Inspector Calls
J. D. Salinger	The Catcher in the Rye
William Shakespeare	Antony and Cleopatra
William Shakespeare	As You Like It
William Shakespeare	Hamlet
William Shakespeare	Henry IV Part I
William Shakespeare	Julius Caesar
William Shakespeare	King Lear
William Shakespeare	Macbeth
William Shakespeare	Measure for Measure
William Shakespeare	The Merchant of Venice
William Shakespeare	A Midsummer Night's Dream
William Shakespeare	Much Ado about Nothing
William Shakespeare	Othello
William Shakespeare	Richard II
William Shakespeare	Romeo and Juliet
William Shakespeare	The Tempest
William Shakespeare	Twelfth Night
George Bernard Shaw	Pygmalion
Alan Sillitoe	Selected Fiction
John Steinbeck	Of Mice and Men and The Pearl
Jonathan Swift	Gulliver's Travels
Dylan Thomas	Under Milk Wood
Alice Walker	The Color Purple
W. B. Yeats	Selected Poetry

ENGLISH COURSEWORK BOOKS

Terri Apter	Women and Society
Kevin Dowling	Drama and Poetry
Philip Gooden	Conflict
Philip Gooden	Science Fiction
Margaret K. Gray	Modern Drama
Graham Handley	Modern Poetry
Graham Handley	Prose
Graham Handley	Childhood and Adolescence
R. J. Sims	The Short Story